W9-AQT-661

TWAYNE'S WORLD AUTHORS SERIES

A Survey of the World's Literature

Sylvia E. Bowman, Indiana University

GENERAL EDITOR

FRANCE

Maxwell A. Smith, Guerry Professor of French, Emeritus
The University of Chattanooga
Former Visiting Professor in Modern Languages
The Florida State University

EDITOR

Paul Verlaine

(TWAS 158)

TWAYNE'S WORLD AUTHORS SERIES (TWAS)

The purpose of TWAS is to survey the major writers—novelists, dramatists, historians, poets, philosophers, and critics—of the nations of the world. Among the national literatures covered are those of Australia, Canada, China, Eastern Europe, France, Germany, Greece, Italy, Japan, Latin America, New Zealand, Poland, Russia, Scandinavia, Spain, and the African nations, as well as Hebrew, Yiddish, and Latin Classical literature. This survey is complemented by Twayne's United States Authors Series and English Authors Series.

The intent of each volume in these series is to present a critical analytical study of the works of the writer; to include biographical and historical material that may be necessary for understanding, appreciation, and critical appraisal of the writer; and to present all material in clear, concise English—but not to vitiate the scholarly content of the work by doing so.

Paul Verlaine

By A. E. CARTER

University of Georgia

Twayne Publishers, Inc. :: New York

Library of Congress Catalog Card Number: 77-120516

MANUFACTURED IN THE UNITED STATES OF AMERICA

TO
HARRY STEINHAUER

Contents

ABOUT THE AUTHOR

A. E. Carter was born in Victoria, B. C. Canada, and educated at the University of British Columbia, McGill University and King's College, University of London. He is at present Professor of French literature at the University of Georgia. His other publications include: *The Idea of Decadence in French Literature*, *Baudelaire et la critique française (1868-1917)*, and *Verlaine: A Study in Parallels.*

Preface

The following study is an attempt to provide students and general readers with an introduction to the work of Paul Verlaine. When he died in Paris on January 8, 1896, he was usually considered the greatest French poet of his time. Many people preferred him to Baudelaire; Mallarmé was the oracle of a small circle; Rimbaud's fame was just beginning. Since then he has undergone something of an eclipse. He is still read, and the anthologies have never dared ignore him, but his poetry is little discussed. With the passage of time and the strains and stresses of twentieth-century living, his plaintive songs no longer feed our disquiet in the same way as the tragic visions of Baudelaire or the volcanic experimentalism of Rimbaud. He appears a lesser man.

On the whole, this situation is not unjust, and I have made no effort to reverse it. But the word "lesser," when used in comparison with Baudelaire and Rimbaud, still means something very considerable. And in several ways (lyric power, mystic inspiration), Verlaine was equal if not superior to Baudelaire and Rimbaud and to most other writers of verse. Just why, with such advantages, he was not altogether greater remains the essential problem. I have discussed it; I have advanced certain theories. They have pertinency, but I should be the last to pretend that they are above criticism. The root of the matter, the explanation for his success and failure, lies in the close relationship between the man and his art. One is a reflection of the other, and as far as possible, I have attempted to show how each of his books was the fruit of a moment in his life: the crisis of adolescence, his marriage, his relations with Rimbaud, the experience of prison and conversion, Lucien Létinois, the squalor of his last years. He stressed the importance of these factors himself, and in evaluating such a man, it is often wise to take the hints he lets drop.

All information on Verlaine has probably not yet been published. V. P. Underwood and Georges Zayed have recently produced brilliant studies based on hitherto unknown material; other documents of this kind must still exist. I was able to consult a few myself. M. Yvan Christ put at my disposal some letters and documents in the possession of his family concerning Verlaine's son, Georges. They complete what we already knew of the alcoholic strain in the Verlaine blood. I have printed them as appendix to a more detailed examination of this and other problems (*Verlaine: A Study in Parallels,* University of Toronto Press). It is doubtful, however, whatever discoveries the future may hold, whether the general picture will change much; we now have the essentials. Verlaine was frequently deplorable, both as man and poet, but his faults are bound up with his genius. The drinking and the brawls, like the occasional lapses of taste and resulting bad verse, arose from a sensibility exquisitely alive to the least seduction. And from the same source flowed the keen, neurotic music of his best poetry. We cannot have one without the other.

A. E. C.

Athens, Georgia
January, 1970

Chronology

1798 Nicolas-Auguste Verlaine born at Paliseul, Belgian Luxemburg.

1809 Elisa-Julie-Josèphe-Stéphanie Dehée, born at Fampoux (Pas-de-Calais).

1831 December 15: they marry.

1844 March 30: Paul-Marie Verlaine born at Metz.

1851 Captain Verlaine resigns from the French Army and moves his family to Paris.

1853 April 17: birth of Mathilde Mauté, Paul Verlaine's future wife.

1854 October 20: Birth of Jean-Arthur Rimbaud, at Charleville in the Ardennes.

1853-1862 Paul Verlaine's school years (Institution Landry, Lycée Bonaparte). Chums: Edmond Lepelletier, Charles de Sivry, Lucien Viotti. During summer vacations of 1861 and 1862, Verlaine begins drinking.

1862 Passes summer with his cousin, Elisa Dujardin, at Lécluze.

1863 Begins to frequent Parnassian circles.

1864 March: position in civil service, Hôtel de Ville de Paris.

1865 November 16-30: article on Baudelaire in *L'Art*. December 30: Captain Nicolas-Auguste Verlaine dies.

1866 March: first number of *le Parnasse contemporain*. Seven of Verlaine's poems appear in the ninth number. November 17:*Poèmes saturniens*.

1867 February 16: death of Elisa Dujardin. Verlaine drunk for three days. End December: *Les Amies* (Brussels).

1868 Verlaine a frequent guest at Nina de Callias' soirées. May 6: *Les Amies* suppressed by court order.

1869 March 22: death of Verlaine's aunt, Mme Grandjean. April: *Fêtes galantes*. June: Verlaine introduced to Charles de Sivry's half-sister, Mathilde Mauté. He begins *La Bonne*

Chanson in her honor. July 18: Victoire Bertrand, Mme Verlaine's maid, writes a description of his violent conduct when drunk. October: engaged to Mathilde Mauté.

1870 Winter and spring: *La Bonne Chanson* completed. July 19: Franco-Prussian War. August 11: Verlaine and Mathilde Mauté are married. September 4: The Third Republic proclaimed. Siege of Paris by the Prussians. November 29: Death of Lucien Viotti. Verlaine joines National Guard, heavy drinking: his relations with his wife begin to deteriorate.

1871 January: armistice. March: the Paris Commune, which Verlaine joins. June: Paris falls to Adolphe Thiers' army from Versailles. Verlaine flees with Mathilde to Fampoux. September: they return to Paris. Verlaine receives two letters from Arthur Rimbaud. September 10: Rimbaud arrives in Paris. October 30: birth of George Verlaine.

1872 January 13: brutal scene between Verlaine and his wife. Her father takes her away to Périgueux. She refuses to return until Rimbaud leaves Paris. March: Rimbaud goes back to Charleville. Mathilde returns to Paris. May: Rimbaud once more in Paris. Fresh scenes between Verlaine and Mathilde. July 7: Rimbaud and Verlaine go to Brussels. July 22: Mathilde follows; her husband refuses to return to Paris with her. She applies for legal separation. September 7: Rimbaud and Verlaine in London.

1873 April 4: Rimbaud and Verlaine in Brussels again. They separate briefly. May 19: Verlaine completes *Romances sans paroles* and sends the manuscript to Lepelletier. End May: Verlaine returns to London with Rimbaud. July 3: violent quarrel. Verlaine goes to Brussels. His mother joins him. July 8: Rimbaud arrives. July 10: Verlaine fires two shots at him because he wants to go to Paris alone. Is arrested the same day. August 8: Verlaine condemned to two years penal servitude. October 25: transferred from the Petits-Carmes prison (Brussels) to the penitentiary (Mons).

1874 March: *Romances sans paroles* published. Mathilde obtains legal separation. June: Verlaine announces his conversion to the prison chaplain. September 8: he sends Lepelletier the sonnet-sequence "Mon Dieu m'a dit."

1875 January 16: discharged from penitentiary. Spends two weeks in a Trappist monastery. Beginning of March: meets Rimbaud at Stuttgart. Violent quarrel. March 20: London. Verlaine obtains a teaching position at Stickney and begins writing poems for *Sagesse* (several of them evocatory of Rimbaud).

1876 Leaves Stickney for Boston (England). In September, he obtains a position at Saint Aloysius College, Bournemouth. More poems for *Sagesse*.

1877 September: returns to France. Obtains position at Collège Notre-Dame de Rethel.

1878 Georges Verlaine sick. Verlaine sees him twice. Meets Lucien Létinois, a student in his English class.

1879 August: Lucien and Verlaine in England. Christmas scene in London. Return to France, end of December.

1880 March, Verlaine buys farm for Létinois family, Coulommes. Completes *Sagesse* and *Voyage en France par un Français*.

1882 Farm bankrupt (January). Verlaine in Paris, July; welcomed by literary circles.

1883 April 7: Lucien dies of typhoid. July 30, Elisa buys Létinois farm at Malval, near Coulommes. August 24, *Les Poètes maudits*. Verlaine and his mother at Malval. Heavy drinking.

1884 May: Huysmans' *A Rebours:* favorable criticism of Verlaine.

1885 January 3: *Jadis et Naguère*. February 9: Mathilde obtains divorce. February 11: Verlaine threatens to kill his mother. Condemned to a year in prison and 500 francs fine. Serves only six weeks. May-June: vagabondage in Coulommes region. Mid-June: rejoins Elisa, Cour Saint-François, Paris. September: bedridden with hydarthrosis.

1886 January 21: Elisa dies. July 22: first hospitalization (henceforth, constantly in and out of hospital). October 30: Mathilde remarries. November: *Mémoires d'un veuf*. Meets Cazals.

1887 April: begins *Bonheur*.

1888 March 26: *Amour*. August: Cazals refuses Verlaine's advances.

1889 End of August: second edition of *Sagesse*. October 26: *Parallèlement*.

1890 March 15: new edition of *Poèmes saturniens. Femmes* (clandestine publication, dated Brussels, 1891).

1891 *Bonheur,* early May. Since 1887, relations with Philomène Boudin and Eugénie Krantz. Autumn: writes *Hombres* at Hôpital Broussais. November 10: Rimbaud dies at Marseilles. December 26: *Chansons pour Elle.*

1892 March 19: *Hombres* completed. April 16: *Liturgies intimes.* November 2-14: lecture tour, Holland.

1893 February 25-March 27: lecture tour in Belgium. May 5: *Elégies.* May 6: *Odes en son honneur.* November 3-9: lecture tour, Nancy and Lunéville. November 19-December 6: lecture tour, England.

1894 May 26: *Dans les Limbes.* August: elected Prince des Poètes. December 1: last sojourn in hospital. December 15: *Epigrammes.* December 22: new edition of *Dédicaces.*

1895 May 15: *Les Confessions.* Autumn: articles on Rimbaud. December: last poem, "Mort!"

1896 January 8: dies at 7:00 P.M. January 10: Interred in family vault at Batignolles.

1914 Mathilde Mauté, former Madame Paul Verlaine, dies at Nice.

1926 Georges Verlaine dies in Paris.

CHAPTER 1

First Years, First Works (1844-1871)

LATE in August, 1871, Paul Verlaine returned to Paris with his wife after three months in the country. It had been no pleasure trip but an escape from possible arrest. He had joined the Commune during the siege of Paris earlier in the year; even after a summer in hiding he was afraid to return to his old address and thought it best to move in with his wife's parents. An unpleasant situation, but far from desperate. Too many Frenchmen were in like case. At that moment in history, when Adolphe Thiers' government was trying to restore order after a disastrous war and an even more disastrous civil conflict, there was a reign of terror in the capital, and arrests totaled thousands. Amidst such chaos Verlaine might hope to be overlooked, as in fact happened; and politics aside, his life appeared settled and even respectable. He was twenty-seven; he had sown his wild oats like any other young writer and ended by making an eligible marriage the previous year. Though he no longer had a job (he had dropped his civil-service position at the City Hall when he fled in June), his mother was well-to-do and always ready to help him. If he could survive the present crisis all would be well: some of his friends like Edmond Lepelletier, even more deeply involved in the Commune than he, later made successful careers under the Third Republic. He had three books of verse in print, all charming and none so original as to be dangerous. It was true that a short time before (1867) he had published a slim volume of Lesbian sonnets, *Les Amies,* which the courts had duly suppressed. But this could be dismissed as a youthful indiscretion. His latest collection, *La Bonne Chanson,* was an exquisite series of odes to his fiancée. If he settled down, produced a book a year, and cultivated the right circles, he could expect in time an established reputation—perhaps even a seat in the Académie

Française. All this was possible had he not found awaiting him in Paris two letters from an unknown correspondent in the Ardennes who signed himself Arthur Rimbaud.

The ensuing catastrophe was so complete that it must have been prepared in advance. We have to look back for an explanation, to the first years of Verlaine's career and the circumstances that made him the man he was in 1871 and the poet he later became. They hardly account for his genius, but without them he would never have written as he did, nor have thrown himself away on a sentimental adventure.

I *Themes and Variations*

In an introductory poem to his first volume he said that he was one of those governed throughout life by the logic of a malignant power:

> Leur plan de vie étant dessiné ligne à ligne
> Par la logique d'une Influence maligne.[1]

A Romantic sentiment, with echoes of the Fatal Man: dozens of poets had already said as much. But in Verlaine's case it was literally true, although he may not have been aware of the fact. There was not one "influence" but two: the irresistible force of heredity and the equally decisive power of upbringing and environment.

He was born at Metz on March 30, 1844, the son of Captain Nicolas-Auguste Verlaine, a career officer in the Engineers, and Elisa Stéphanie Dehée, daughter of rich sugar refiners from Fampoux in the Pas-de-Calais. A union of this sort, army and bourgeoisie, usually means respectability at its dullest: years of garrison duty and army friends, leading to retirement and a pension. And while Nicolas-Auguste lived, such was his household. But there were skeletons in the family closets, ghosts of dead men and old scandals; and modern research, ruthless as ever, has brought them all to light. Like Paul himself, the captain was perhaps ignorant of their existence. He had lost his father at seven and been soldiering ever since he was sixteen—a self-reliant, practical man, little given to brooding over the past, his own or others'. His mother's family had reared him—the Grandjeans: landed proprietors in close touch with the army and the Church. They were not the sort of people to tell him that his father and grandfather on the Verlaine side had been notorious drunks, whose sprees led to clashes with the law.[2] Nineteenth-century families preferred to leave such details in decent obscurity. To us, however, this background is interesting in many ways. It reads like an advance sketch of Paul Verlaine's own career: drink, temper, violence, and police intervention. And we find a last manifestation of it in the life of his son Georges—incarcerated for drunken brawling in 1904 and described by an attendant physician as "a simple case of hereditary alcoholism."[3] A tendency which afflicts five generations, skipping only one, Nicolas-Auguste, is clearly significant in explaining a man's character and, if he is a poet, the verse he writes.

Had the mother provided qualities of balance and sanity, the paternal taint might have been neutralized. But in some ways Elisa Dehée's contribution was even more sinister than her husband's. Her longing for motherhood was so ardent that it verged on the morbid, and during the first thirteen years of marriage it was cruelly tried: three miscarriages occurred. The situation was beyond her powers of adjustment: she had the foetuses preserved in alcohol and stored them in a cupboard. Even allowing for the sentimental necrophilia of the period, this was an extraordinary habit. Nicolas-Auguste was often posted from one garrison to another (Metz in 1844, Montpellier in 1845, Sète, Nìmes and Metz again from 1846 to 1849), and house-moving was much more complicated than it is now. The spectacle of a woman in the prime of life—she was thirty-five when Paul was born—crossing France with items of this sort in her trunks suggests much, helps account for the intense love she bore her one living child: a love that survived years of abuse, including at least one attempt at murder, and led her from comfortable respectability to poverty and death in a bawdy house.

From the moment of his birth, Paul was the center of her existence. The old phrase, "he could do no wrong," fits the situation perfectly. She raised him in a debilitating atmosphere of absolute devotion. "She was so blinded by maternal love that she lost all moral sense," her daughter-in-law noted acidly. Even the comment of a friendly witness is not much more favorable: "She adored her Paul, spoiled him, pardoned everything he did. In later years she often had reason to regret her too great indulgence, and she suffered in silence the boy's misbehavior, never daring to scold him."[4]

The worst thing about an experience of this kind is that no man who has had it would wish matters otherwise. He may understand that it was a poison which debased his will and corrupted his imagination, but he loves the poison. In after life he is perpetually obsessed by memories and regrets for the what-has-been: the past fastens onto the present like a malignant growth, dwarfing and retarding. He knows, if only subconsciously, that he received more than he gave and more than he could possibly deserve, and at the moment of puberty his sexual instincts are subtly warped. He reaches manhood with an obscure sense of guilt, turns reticent and masochistic, forever seeking a mother substitute and turning to the euphoria of debauch when his search is frustrated. Sexual promiscuity is much more to him than mere physical indulgence. It becomes an expiation, a complicated form of self-punishment, assuming depraved or satanic overtones inasmuch as the maternal image is violated or evaded. And if such a man is a writer, his books become records of sentimental failure—descriptions of his mishaps in pursuit of a hopeless ideal or lingering accounts of deliberate self-abasement. He lives on his nerves, in a perverted dependence on sensory impressions. Reality fascinates him in exaggerated and contradictory ways, suggesting that somewhere, somehow, he will find again the paradise symbolized by his childhood. Each adventure on which he embarks is a light-flecked, shimmering path which leads, not to an Eden of realized illusions, but to quagmire and dead-end. Bad as the resulting trauma is, it becomes immeasurably worse when embarrassed by a craving for drink. One tendency compliments the other: if dream and illusion fail, there is always alcohol, the mighty panacea, the unfailing vehicle of escape. We can follow these alterations of crisis and drink, drink and crisis throughout Verlaine's career. At every stage he was dominated by forces beyond his control: the taint inherited from his father and his mother's remorseless love.

II *Childhood and Youth*

The *Confessions* he wrote at the end of his life supply a number of curious revelations—all the more interesting when we recall that the book was written by a man of fifty, an age which usually implies maturity. Yet this is just the quality we do not find. The book covers the years up to Rimbaud's advent; and though Verlaine speaks in the final pages of continuing it later, nothing further ever appeared. Time was lacking, of course; when the volume was published in 1894 he was within eighteen months of the grave. But it is unlikely that he would have added much, even had he lived another decade. There was nothing much left to add. The essential qualities of his nature, the emotional habits from which his poetry sprang, were all formed during his first twenty-seven years, and most of them belong to the beginning of that period rather than to its end. No one better illustrates than Verlaine the truth of the old saw that the boy is father to the man.

Fundamentally, the book is a dreamy recall of childhood, a sentimental reverie which, however exact it may be in many ways, bears little relevancy to the facts. Verlaine even calls it "a fairy tale,"[5] and the phrase is only half ironical. But the discrepancy between truth and fancy is not the important point. What matters is that such was the past as he recalled it, a never-never land of the imagination. From this point of view, the world sketched in the *Confessions* was more real than if every detail had been rigorously exact. Memories of the father and mother dominate many pages: "I was proud of my father's handsome uniform . . . and of the splendid way he carried himself. . . . He had a martial yet gentle face, with a habit of authority left by years of command which never failed to impress me."—"My poor mother, overcome by my tumultuous adolescence and later by my even worse maturity, used to say: 'You'll see: you'll go so far that one day I'll run off and you'll never be able to find out where I am . . .' I often dream of her: we quarrel, I know I'm wrong, I'm on the point of admitting my faults and begging her to forgive me, confessing how much I love her, how much I regret causing her pain . . . and she's vanished! The rest of the dream is lost in the increasing anguish of a useless and infinite search."

There is also the recollection of his first communion: "I felt then, for the first time, that almost physical presence which all communicants experience . . . God is there, in our flesh and in our blood."[6] Religion and the sense of protection and forgiveness it provides was closely allied to recollections of his parents: his subsequent conversion, after years of skepticism and free living, was a return to the earlier peace.

It is not surprising that, with such a background, he was fatally ill-fitted to cope with ordinary living, as an incident of his ninth year shows. Captain Verlaine had resigned his commission and moved the family to Paris in 1851; he entered Paul at boarding school, the Institution Landry, two years later. The rough-and-tumble of the place terrified the child. "The other boys filled me with horror—not fear, horror."[7] Completely disoriented, he could think of nothing but escape. When he reached home, his father refused to yield to this tantrum and had him taken back next day. But the episode reveals how the child's emotional patterns had become fixed. And fixed they remained. Whenever the adult Verlaine found himself facing an insoluble problem (marriage, Rimbaud, the death of Létinois), he ran away—across land and water or, if that was impossible, into the nearest bar. Over thirty years later, when he wrote a sketch of himself as "Pauvre Lelian," he recalled these events and noted their importance: "Exceptional parents—an excellent father, a charming mother—spoiled him as an only son. The downfall began at boarding-school, where he was sent early. I can still see him in his long black blouse . . . leaning on the fence that separated the two playgrounds, weeping almost, amongst the other children. . . . That same evening he escaped and was taken back next day, by dint of cakes and promises."[8] *A force de gâteaux et de promesses:* he could not have described the situation better. Cakes and promises were something he could never afterwards forego.

Not all his school experiences were equally negative. He graduated from the Institution Landry to the Lycée Bonaparte (now Condorcet) in 1855, and soon grew accustomed to classroom and dormitory; he even made lasting friendships there: Edmond Lepelletier, his future biographer; Charles de Sivry, whose half-sister he eventually married. And Lucien Viotti, a less obvious relationship, but even more decisive in other ways. School life also provided opportunities for sexual discovery which he could hardly have known in the closed circle of a family. Boys living in groups usually pool knowledge of this kind; and a great city like Paris is an education in itself. The experience is not particularly demoralizing, however startling some of its manifestations may appear: the normal adolescent takes them in his stride. But Paul

Verlaine was not a normal adolescent, and the influence of his sheltered life and his mother's doting care soon revealed itself in complex ways. As the *Confessions* show, the neurotic habits of childhood carried his sexual cravings far beyond the average pubescent urge. By the time he was seventeen he was frequenting brothels. The habit is not unusual, but his reasons for indulging it unquestionably were: "Cheap prostitutes obsessed me, I had them in my blood. If a decent woman . . . had offered herself, I'd have asked her to let me alone."—"I continued my experiments with a frequency which only increased my curiosity, and my curiosity is still unsatisfied even now when I'm over fifty."[9]

It was less the prostitutes he had in his blood than Elisa; the term "experiments" tells us more than Verlaine himself understood. Like most men touched by neurosis, he was highly keyed to sexual stimulation: pure lechery, a frank enjoyment of all types of sexual contact, dominated him at each stage of his life: in this respect his last poems are as revealing as his first ("even now when I'm over fifty"—he died at fifty-two): no one ever described in more telling detail the erotic potentialities of the flesh. Yet lechery, as such, was not his main problem: in like cases it rarely is. He was facing something more intricate: his guilt feelings and the masochism they engendered. Desire was bound up with the mother image. He wanted to enjoy, but also to atone for his enjoyment. And lust—the physical ability to perform this or that action—could only function in a vacuum divorced from all recollections of Elisa. And what could be less like her than the blowzy inmate of a *maison-close?* His affairs with prostitutes were indeed "experiments," keenly relished sensations complicated by self-torture; and also (especially when abetted by drink) vehicles of evasion. Debauchery, whether alcoholic or sexual, liberates the individual from his burdens or remorse and recollection. The past is abolished: however briefly, he achieves a state of free will, inhabits a zone of pure fantasy unprobed by the searching beams of reflection and intelligence.

This imbalance was further perplexed by another factor: during his school years Verlaine made his first contact with homosexuality. For most boys the experience is unimportant, soon forgotten as they become interested in women. But Verlaine was emotionally involved: his partners inspired him with warmer feelings than friendship, and since they belonged to his own sex, they were even less like Elisa than were the trollops of the brothel. The tendency grew stronger as his teens passed: we cannot say whether it was latent or acquired. But certainly if it depended on nothing more than school-boy habits, it is strange that throughout Verlaine's adult life his most violent and lasting passions were homosexual: Viotti, Rimbaud, Létinois, Cazals. And in each one, he sought much more than sexual gratification: "Love me, protect me, and give me confidence," he wrote Rimbaud in 1872. "Since I'm a very weak person, I have great need of kindness."[10] With slight variations, he said the same things to all those he loved, his wife included; and relationships of this sort, based on psychic weakness, usually end badly. The stronger partner finds himself yoked to an emotional imbecile, eternally demanding solicitude and concessions. Affection breaks down into exasperation on one side and lachrymose recriminations on the other. The problem has no solution, it can only be evaded. Hence Verlaine's sexual crises usually coincided with bouts of drinking. He says himself that his first real drunk occurred when he was seventeen or eighteen,[11] and it was just at this time that the full implications of his sexual cravings dawned upon him, a point I shall discuss in a moment.

III *Literary Contacts. The Parnassians*

He graduated from Bonaparte in 1862 and two years later found a civil-service appointment at the Hôtel de Ville. It paid 1800 francs a year, which by 1870 had risen to 3000. The duties were easy, and since he lived with his parents at minimum expense, he had money and leisure to do as he pleased. Lepelletier and De Sivry introduced him to a number of literary figures, one of whom, Louis-Xavier de Ricard, had founded a journal, *L'Art.* It changed its name to *Le Parnasse contemporain* in 1866, and in its pages Verlaine first began to publish.

The poets grouped around the new periodical have been known ever since as "Parnassians." Literary history needs such terms, but it must be admitted that this label is even more unsatisfactory than most. *Le Parnasse contemporain* printed writers as diverse as Théodore de Banville, Baudelaire, Leconte de Lisle, Heredia, Mallarmé, and Verlaine himself. A school made up of such varied talents would be rich indeed; and a brief glance through their work is enough to reveal that they had little in common—perhaps only one thing: without being anti-Romantic (they all admired Victor Hugo), they did represent a kind of reaction against certain Romantic tendencies, particularly the personal, confessional style of writing and its neglect of technical discipline in favor of feeling and inspiration. Some Parnassians (Gautier, Banville, Leconte de Lisle) had been producing for many years and already had established reputations; when they contributed to *Le Parnasse contemporain* they had no thought of forming a school. But French literature likes to move in schools, and in this sense the new magazine was convenient: it gave a name to a tendency otherwise hard to define. With the passage of time, the epithet has become attached to a few poets only—Gautier and Banville, and especially Leconte de Lisle and Heredia. When we discuss Parnassianism it is their work we mean, plastic rather than musical, taking ideas from Greek paganism rather than from the mediaeval or Renaissance Christianity dear to the Romantics, and above all "impersonal." The adjective was a favorite with the Parnassians. They painted and described without comment, and their own emotions were kept strictly in the background.[12]

IV Poèmes saturniens *(1866)*

As his subsequent work proved, Verlaine had small talent for poetry of this kind. But he did his best to write it in his first collection. "My brand of Leconte de Lisle, spiced up with Baudelaire," he defined the book some thirty years afterwards.[13] It has four divisions, *Melancholia, Eaux-fortes, Paysages tristes* and *Caprices,* and the imitations of Leconte de Lisle are in fact so complete as to be almost docile, especially in the "Prologue" and the "Epilogue" with which the volume opens and closes. The first is a declaration of Parnassian faith. During the great periods of Greece, India, and the Middle Ages, we are told, poetry and action were one: poets sang the exploits of heroes. The theory is buttressed with frequent references to Hindu and Greek mythology: Raghû, Kchatrya, Rama, Valmiki, plus the inevitable "Néant divin," the divine annihilation of Sanskrit lore which the Parnassians saw as an approximation of their own cult of impassivity.[14] The effect is somewhat heavy. These exotic names do not read well in French, and even worse are the Greek names, written according to Leconte de Lisle's formula in direct transliteration from the original tongue: Alkaïos, Homéros, Hektor, Akhilleus, Arès instead of the usual Alcée, Homère, Hector, Achille, Mars, and so on. It was Verlaine's first venture into pedantry, and fortunately it was also his last. The conclusion of the poem is that in modern times Dream and Action are separate and must remain so. Nineteenth-century poets live in isolation from the contemporary world, and far from attempting to mix with it, they should retreat even further into haughty solitude: "The world, disturbed by their deep message, exiles them. In their turn, they exile the world! . . . The love of Beauty is the Poet's faith, the Azure his standard, and the Ideal his law! Ask him nothing more, for his gaze cannot abase itself for so much as an hour to the shameful level of vulgar needs."

> Le monde, que troublait leur parole profonde,
> Les exile. A leur tour ils exilent le monde!
> . . . .
> Le Poëte, l'amour du Beau, voilà sa foi,
> L'Azur, son étendard, et l'Idéal, sa loi!
> Ne lui demandez rien de plus, car ses prunelles, . . .
> Ne sauraient s'abaisser une heure seulement
> Sur le honteux conflit des besognes vulgaires.

The "Epilogue" sums up the idea and formulates a new esthetic creed. Facile inspiration, the guiding principle of Romanticism, is renounced: "We have always distrusted Inspiration . . . Ah! Inspiration: one invokes it at sixteen! But what we need now, Supreme Poets that we are, we who venerate the Gods without believing in them . . . we who polish our words like precious chalices and who write moving verses in cold blood, we who are never seen in harmonious groups languishing of an evening on the shores of *lakes*"—a hit at Lamartine's famous "Le Lac"—"What we need during our hours of study . . . is Obstinacy and Will Power! . . . Ceaseless study, unheard-of effort, unparalleled combat . . . Let the Inspired Poets, their hearts inflamed by a mere glance, abandon themselves to the winds like birches: poor wretches! Art does not consist of dissipating one's soul: Is the Venus de Milo made of marble or not?"

Ah! l'Inspiration, on l'invoque à seize ans!
Ce qu'il nous faut à nous, les Suprêmes Poëtes
Qui vénérons les Dieux et qui n'y croyons pas . . .
A nous qui ciselons les mots comme des coupes
Et qui faisons des vers émus très froidement,
A nous qu'on ne voit point les soirs aller par groupes
Harmonieux au bord des *lacs* et nous pâmant,
Ce qu'il nous faut, à nous, c'est, aux lueurs des lampes,
La science conquise et le sommeil dompté . . .
C'est l'Obstination et c'est la Volonté! . . .
Ce qu'il nous faut à nous, c'est l'étude sans trêve,
C'est l'effort inouï, le combat nonpareil . . .
Libre à nos Inspirés, coeurs qu'une oeillade enflamme,
D'abandonner leur être aux vents comme un bouleau;
Pauvres gens! l'Art n'est pas d'éparpiller son ame:
Est-elle en marbre, ou non, la Vénus de Milo?

In poems like "Un Dahlia" and "Çavitri" he tried to write according to these precepts. The dahlia is described as a "hard-breasted courtesan," odorless and impassive, throning like an idol in formal perfection. "Çavitri" is a Hindu legend: to save her husband, a wife swore to remain for three days and nights motionless and kept her vow: "Let us therefore be as impassive as Çavitri, but, like her, let us keep in our souls a high ideal":

Ainsi que Çavitri faisons-nous impassibles,
Mais, comme elle, dans l'âme ayons un haut dessein.

"César Borgia" and "La Mort de Philippe II" are Parnassian treatments of well-worn Romantic themes. The great Romantic poets had always been fascinated by the lurid personalities of the sixteenth century; and Verlaine's lines, besides their borrowings from Leconte de Lisle, owe much to works like Hugo's *Lucrèce Borgia* and "La Rose de l'Infante." "Historic and heroic subjects," he called them afterward, "an epic or didactic tone which I naturally took from Victor Hugo and even more directly from M. Leconte de Lisle."[15] Like the rest of his Romantic and Parnassian efforts, they are neither very good nor very bad: a high level of competent mediocrity. Yet though Parnassianism never inspired his best poetry, it cannot be dismissed as irrelevant. We find too many traces of it in his work and thought down to the extreme limit of his career. The *Paysages belges* section of *Romances sans paroles*, for example, completed in 1872, consists of "impersonal" descriptions of towns and landscapes. A year later (May 16, 1873) he wrote Lepelletier: "I'm caressing the idea of writing a book of poems . . . from which *man* will be completely absent. Landscapes, things, the malice of things, the goodness of things. Here are a few titles: *Life in the Attic*, *Underwater.*, *The Island*. Each poem will have from 300 to 400 lines. The verse will be written according to a system I'm going to perfect. *Life in the Attic* in the style of Rembrandt; *Underwater*, a real song of Undine; *The Island*, a big flower-picture, etc., etc. Don't laugh until you know my system. I've perhaps stumbled on a very good idea." Fourteen years after this (October 23, 1887) he told another correspondent: "I'm caressing the idea . . . of writing long and short impersonal poems." And during an interview with Count Kessler on July 26, 1895, he said that "he would still like to be 'impassive' in his work, like Leconte de Lisle."[16] This was less than six months before he died. A theory which haunts a man for so long must be something more than mere youthful infatuation. Was it the seduction of opposites? Or a genuine talent that never reached complete expression?

However this may be, Baudelaire's influence was, on the whole, more fortunate. Verlaine first read *Les Fleurs du Mal* when he was fourteen at the Lycée Bonaparte; and during the next six or eight years he went through all his predecessor's works—artistic and literary criticism, translations of Poe, etc. seeking what best suited his own needs. What he found is set forth in an essay he wrote on Baudelaire about the time he was completing *Poèmes saturniens*. He notes how the older poet was in agreement with the Parnassians in his refusal to confound Art and morality: "Yes, Art is independent of Morals and politics, Philosophy and Science. . . . The end of Poetry is beauty, Beauty alone, pure Beauty, with no alloy of Usefulness, Truth or Justice."[17] A creed he never afterwards renounced.

Even more important were the ways Baudelaire differed from the reigning school. He composed verse that was recognizably contemporary in feeling and setting, in a style totally free of Greek and Hindu bric-a-brac. This fact struck Verlaine at once. "The profound originality of Charles Baudelaire, I believe, lies in representing modern man. . . . The physical modern man, as he has been formed by the refinements of an excessive civilization. . . . Take the love-poems of *Les Fleurs du Mal:* Love, in Baudelaire's verse, is indeed love as a Parisian of the nineteenth century must feel it: something feverish and analytical at the same time: pure passion is mixed with reflection." Typical examples, he notes, are "Semper eadem," "L'Aube spirituelle," "Une Charogne," "Parfum exotique," "La Chevelure," "Je t'adore à l'égale," "Le Serpent qui danse," "Une nuit que j'étais près," "Le Poison," and "Sonnet d'automne."[18]

If we turn to the erotic numbers of *Poèmes saturniens* (there are eight, grouped under the general title of *Melancholia*, although "Sérénade" and "Il Bacio" which come later, belong to the same category) we find echoes of Baudelaire in line after line. The brilliant young disciple wanted to honor his master with a skillful imitation, wanted to write both "feverishly" and "analytically." His relative ill-success arose from differences in temperament rather than lack of talent: he was instinctive, sensitive, emotional; he had none of Baudelaire's remorseless lucidity. The sonnet "Lassitude" is a good instance: he was attempting something analogous to Baudelaire's "Sonnet d'automne"; the results show clearly how one poet differed from the other.

Here are Baudelaire's lines:

> Ils me disent, tes yeux, clairs comme le cristal:
> "Pour toi, bizarre amant, quel est donc mon mérite?"
> —Sois charmante et tais-toi! Mon coeur, que tout irrite,
> Excepté la candeur de l'antique animal,
>
> Ne veut pas te montrer son secret infernal,
> Berceuse dont la main aux longs sommeils m'invite,
> Ni sa noire légende avec la flamme écrite.
> Je hais la passion et l'esprit me fait mal!
>
> Aimons-nous doucement. L'Amour dans sa guérite,
> Ténébreux, embusqué, bande son arc fatal.
> Je connais les engins de son vieil arsenal:
>
> Crime, horreur et folie!—O pâle marguerite!
> Comme moi n'es-tu pas un soleil automnal,
> O ma si blanche, ô ma si froide Marguerite?

What does this confession of tired sadism become under Verlaine's pen?

> De la douceur, de la douceur, de la douceur!
> Calme un peu ces transports fébriles, ma charmante.
> Même au fort du déduit parfois, vois-tu, l'amante
> Doit avoir l'abandon paisible de la soeur.
>
> Sois langoureuse, fais ta caresse endormante,
> Bien égaux tes soupirs et ton regard berceur.
> Va, l'étreinte jalouse et le spasme obsesseur
> Ne valent pas un long baiser, même qui mente!
>
> Mais dans ton cher coeur d'or, me dis-tu, mon enfant,
> La fauve passion va sonnant l'olifant! . . .
> Laisse-la trompeter à son aise, la gueuse!
>
> Mets ton front sur mon front et ta main dans ma main,
> Et fais-moi des serments que tu rompras demain,
> Et pleurons jusqu'au jour, ô petite fougueuse!

For Verlaine poetry was not a spiritual adventure in search of new experience, but a sort of alchemy, a means of volatilizing reality into illusion and sensation. Charming as verse like "Lassitude" is, it lacks the analytic concision we meet everywhere in *Les Fleurs du Mal.*

The same applies to other examples of Baudelaire's influence. His modernism, for instance, implied a revolutionary shift in decor. Up to the middle of the nineteenth century, most French verse, whether Romantic or Parnassian, was exotic, seeking in space and time landscapes and periods as far removed from the unglamorous present as might be. But when modern man became the subject—"physical modern man, as he has been formed by the refinements of an excessive civilization"—he had to be presented in an environment where he might be best observed, the great city. Most of *Les Fleurs du Mal* are set in Paris, and many passages throughout Baudelaire's prose works show how the metropolis fascinated him. As Verlaine says, until Baudelaire used it, "the city had been less exploited by poets than by novelists. And yet what a poetic theme it is, what a world of comparisons, images and metaphors! What an inexhaustible source of descriptions and reveries! This is what Baudelaire understood: he was essentially a Parisian genius."[19] Several of *Poèmes saturniens* ("Croquis parisien," Crépuscule du soir mystique," "Marco," "Nocturne parisien") are "city" poetry of this kind, and as such they are fairly successful. But they fail on an essential point. For Baudelaire the metropolis was a symbol of man's dual nature, of his greatness and his misery, his infinite capacity for good and evil, achievement and destruction. Verlaine could not handle themes like these; when he looked at Paris he saw little beyond surface detail. The tragic implications turned picturesque or melodramatic: "Roll on your indolent waters, dreary Seine. Under your bridges bathed in sick mists many bodies have passed, dead, horrible, rotten, whose souls were slain by Paris. . . . And you flow on, Seine, and as you crawl, you drag through Paris your muddy old serpent's route—carrying towards your ports cargoes of wood, coal and corpses!"

> Roule, roule ton flot indolent, morne Seine.—
> Sous tes ponts qu'environne une vapeur malsaine
> Bien des corps ont passé, morts, horribles, pourris,
> Dont les âmes avaient pour meurtrier Paris . . .
> Et tu coules toujours, Seine, et, tout en rampant,
> Tu traînes dans Paris ton cours de vieux serpent,
> De vieux serpent boueux, emportant vers tes havres
> Tes cargaisons de bois, de houille et de cadavres!

Baudelaire's example was perhaps best when it pointed the way to certain technical experiments. This point requires elucidation, and I shall discuss it more fully in my last chapter when the time comes to sum up Verlaine's career. For the moment, two points will suffice. Baudelaire weakened the median caesura of the classical alexandrine, a trick known as *enjambement sur la césure,* and he was fond of *rejet,* overflow from one line to the next. Verlaine quotes several examples of these phenomena from *Les Fleurs du Mal,* pointing out that Baudelaire was the first in France to dare lines like the following:

> . . . Pour entendre un de ces concerts riches de cuivre . . .
> . . . Exaspéré comme un ivrogne qui voit double . . .

It is clearly impossible to find a caesural pause after *ces* and *un.*

Similar lines are frequent throughout *Poèmes saturniens,* particularly in the sonnets of *Melancholia.* In each case the caesura is not the true pause:

> . . . Et je baisai sa main / blanche, dévotement . . .
> . . . Ayant poussé la porte / étroite qui chancelle . . .
> . . . De vigne folle avec / les chaises de rotin . . .
> . . . Chaque alouette qui / va et vient m'est connue . . .
> . . . De mes ennuis, de mes / dégoûts, de mes détresses . . .

And so on. One or two poems, like "A une femme" and "L'Angoisse," are almost totally irregular in this respect.

As for *rejet,* Baudelaire used it often. Verlaine refers to one example:

> Tout cassés
> Qu'ils sont . . .

And many others might be found. Verlaine made this technique his own; it became one of the hall-marks of his poetry:

> . . . l'automne
> Faisait voler la grive . . .
> . . . l'humble tonnelle
> De vigne folle . . .
> . . . l'amante
> Doit avoir l'abandon paisible . . .
>
> . . . Elle a
> L'inflexion des voix chères . . .
> . . . Si bien
> Que le gémissement premier du premier homme
> Chassé d'Eden . . .

Innovations of this kind are the chief originality of *Poèmes saturniens;* they were genuinely creative, corresponding to the wilful, irresponsible qualities of Verlaine's nature: a craving for asymmetry, irregularity, and the caprice and freedom they make possible. But he was still too young, too much under the influence of his masters to combine technical innovations with equal liberty of content. The sentiments and phraseology of *Melancholia* are often very banal. "Nevermore" is a mass of clichés: "rayon monotone," "bois jaunissant," the two lovers with "les cheveux et la pensée au vent," the lady's "regard émouvant" and her "voix d'or vivant." Even the title is lifted from Poe's "Raven." "Après trois ans," despite Verlaine's declarations to the contrary in his "Prologue," is a fourteen-line version of Lamartine's "Le Lac"—not to mention Musset's "Souvenir" and Hugo's "Tristesse d'Olympio." Other numbers are veritable centos of Baudelaire. Only twice does the true Verlaine, the Verlaine of the future, show himself. He admitted as much in 1890, when, rereading *Paysages tristes,* he called it "an egg from which a whole flight of singing lines, both vague and definite, has since been hatched, and which I was the first to snare."[20] This is especially true of "Chanson d'automne," certainly one of the finest lyrics in all his work: "The long sobs of the violins of autumn wound my heart with a monotonous languour":

Les sanglots longs
Des violons
De l'automme
Blessent mon coeur
D'une langueur
Montone . . .

Still better, however, is "Mon Rêve familier" of *Melancholia.* Like the rest of the section it has aroused much speculation, and M. J. H. Bornecque has recently suggested that, together with the other sonnets, it was written in honor of Verlaine's cousin, Elisa Moncomble.[21] His parents adopted her eight years before he was born; she grew up with him, became part of his childhood Eden, "one of the tenderest elements," he writes in the *Confessions,* "a little mother alongside my real mother; an authority not sweeter, not dearer, but closer to me, as it were . . . almost an elder sister."[22] He was sixteen when she married Auguste Dujardin, a sugar refiner, and settled at Lécluse near Douai. Verlaine spent two summers at her house, 1862 and 1865. That he loved her is certain, but in what way? *Melancholia* was composed in 1865, and much of it hints at thwarted passion, with the suggestion that three years earlier things had been different. This is the theme of "Après trois ans," and the next poem, "Voeu," is even more explicit: "Here I am, sad and lonely, despairing, colder than an old man, just like an orphan bereft of an elder sister":

> Si que me voilà seul à présent, morne et seul,
> Morne et désespéré, plus glacé qu'un aïeul,
> Et tel qu'un orphelin pauvre sans soeur aînée.

In "A une femme" and "L'Angoisse" the tone rises further: "I suffer, I suffer frightfully. The groans of Adam driven from Eden are mere bucolics beside mine!"—"Tired of living, yet fearing death, just like a brig abandoned to the tides, my soul sets sail for terrible disasters."

> Oh! Je souffre, je souffre affreusement, si bien
> Que le gémissement premier du premier homme
> Chassé d'Eden n'est qu'une églogue au prix du mien!
> . . . .
> Lasse de vivre, ayant peur de mourir, pareille
> Au brick perdu jouet du flux et du reflux,
> Mon âme pour d'affreux naufrages appareille.

Was all this inspired by Elisa? Certain details hardly fit her, like the epithet *petite fougueuse* of "Lassitude." Her figure is perhaps clearer in the concluding lines of "Voeu": "A woman of persuasive and warming love, tender, pensive and brunette, and never offended, who sometimes kisses your forehead as though you were a child":

> O la femme à l'amour câlin et réchauffant,
> Douce, pensive et brune, et jamais étonnée,
> Et qui parfois vous baise au front, comme un enfant!

"Mon Rêve familier" is the culmination of the sequence: "I often have that strange and penetrating dream of an unknown woman whom I love and who loves me, and who is not, each time, quite the same nor quite different, and who loves me and understands me":

> Je fais souvent ce rêve étrange et pénétrant
> D'une femme inconnue, et que j'aime, et qui m'aime

> Et qui n'est, chaque fois, ni tout à fait la même
> Ni tout à fait une autre, et m'aime et me comprend.

It goes without saying, of course, that even supposing Elisa to have been the subject nothing suggests that she returned Verlaine's passion. She was not the sort of woman for an adulterous intrigue with a boy she looked on as a brother. Nor are the young poet's expressions licentious: as so often in his love poetry, they have a flavor of attenuated incest: the lady is a "sister," an "elder sister," a "mother"; she kisses him "as though he were a child"; she is even "unknown," *inconnue,* and this epithet is perhaps the key to the whole matter. The woman in question was a figment of the poet's dream; if Elisa was really involved, then she was little more than a pretext, a catalyst, precipitating a whole universe of nostalgic desire.

Such considerations, however, have small point by comparison with the beauty of the lines. Poems like "Mon Rêve familier" explain Verlaine's stature as a lyric poet. Regrets for lost happiness, refuge in illusion and sensation, subtle harmony, *rejet* and *enjambement*—all combine to create one of those unique works of which, now that a century has passed, we see that he alone possessed the secret. He was to return to this style later, in different circumstances and with a very different content; but in this one sonnet he brought it to perfection, and however fine his subsequent poems may be, none are better.

V Fêtes galantes *(1869)*

Poèmes saturniens was hardly off the press when he began work on a new volume which appeared three years later. It has always been one of his most popular collections, and with reason: nowhere else, not even in *Romances sans paroles* or *Sagesse,* did he write verse of such pure charm, with scarcely one false note.

At first reading, the book gives something of a plastic, Parnassian impression: the light, fantastic Parnassianism of Banville (of whose *Caryatides,* 1846, there are echoes), rather than the heavy seriousness of Leconte de Lisle. Verlaine had turned for inspiration not to India or ancient Greece, but to eighteenth-century painting, particularly the work of Antoine Watteau (1684-1721). A few items in *Poèmes saturniens* suggest the coming change: "Sérénade," "Nuit de Walpurgis classique." The first has a brittle, crystalline music totally at variance with both Parnassianism and the subdued murmurs of "Mon Rêve familier": "Open your soul and your ear to the sound of my mandolin: it's for you that I've made this cruel and wheedling song":

> Ouvre ton âme et ton oreille au son
> De ma mandoline:
> Pour toi j'ai fait, pour toi, cette chanson
> Cruelle et câline.

The "Nuit" is a curious effort to set a Romantic witch-pageant into the gardens of Versailles: "A rhythmical Sabbath, extremely rhythmical. Imagine a garden by Lenôtre. . . . Veiled songs of distant horns in which the tenderness of the senses clasps the soul's terror in an ecstacy of chords harmoniously dissonant; and now as the horns call, white forms suddenly embrace, diaphanous; and the moonlight turns them opalescent in the green shadows of the branches: a Watteau such as Raffet might have dreamed!"[23]

> Un rhythmique sabbat, rhythmique, extrêmement
> Rhythmique.—Imaginez un jardin de Lenôtre . . .
> Des chants voilés des cors lointains où la tendresse
> Des sens étreint l'effroi de l'âme en des accords
> Harmonieusement dissonants dans l'ivresse;
> Et voici qu'à l'appel des cors
> S'entrelacent soudain des formes toutes blanches,
> Diaphanes, et que le clair de lune fait
> Opalines parmi l'ombre verte des branches,
> —Un Watteau rêvé par Raffet!—

All the essentials of *Fêtes galantes* are present: moonlight, colored shadows, veiled eroticism, sinister and alluring music. Even Watteau's name.

He was not, for that matter, the only artistic source of *Fêtes galantes*. Traces may be found of other eighteenth-century painters: Boucher, Nattier, La Tour, Canaletto, Lancret; and there were literary influences as well. Verlaine had read widely and he also liked eighteenth-century music—Favart's operas *(Ninette à la Cour)* which he subsequently utilized in *Romances sans paroles*. Other Parnassians shared his tastes—Gautier, Banville, Mallarmé and Glatigny; there was a stanza praising Watteau in Baudelaire's "Les Phares," and a long poem by Victor Hugo, "La Fête chez Thérèse" *(Les Contemplations,* 1856), which Verlaine knew by heart. Lepelletier calls it the chief inspiration of *Fêtes galantes.*[24]

But the main quality of the new book is less an adaptation of old themes than a sort of iridescent elegance, as elusive as the sheen of an opal; a refinement of style and sense which is very nearly unique in literature. It matters little that Watteau and Lancret painted *fêtes galantes* (an eighteenth-century term meaning something analogous to a garden party). What counts is that Verlaine, transposing their effects into verse, achieved results of which they can scarcely have dreamt. Like all his best work, *Fêtes galantes* is entirely personal: a private universe of sensation. "Local color" it may have—references to this or that eighteenth-century detail. But the over-all impression has little in common with the eighteenth century of history. The reign of Louis XV was robust and positive: it would have shrugged its shoulders over Verlaine's lines. One imagines the sarcasms of Voltaire, the ironic comments of Choiseul or Mme du Deffand. No eighteenth-cenutry artist, least of all Watteau, ever painted moonlight; yet moonlight is the book's very essence, the source of the ambiguous charm. Verlaine's temperament required this doubtful illumination: light reflected, not light direct. "Your soul is a chosen landscape," he writes in the first poem, "Clair de Lune," "where seductive masks and bergamasks pass by, playing the lute, and dancing, and half-sad beneath their fantastic disguises":

> Votre âme est un paysage choisi
> Qui vont charmant masques et bergamasques,
> Jouant du luth, et dansant et quasi
> Tristes sous leurs déguisements fantasques . . .

The piece sets the tone of all that follows: the subtle depiction of a psychic state, alert to the nervous stimulation of color, sound, and music. In "A la promenade," "the sun's beam, attenuated by the shadow of the low lindens along the avenue, comes to us blue and dying as if on purpose"—

Et la lueur du soleil qu'atténue
L'ombre des bas tilleuls de l'avenue
Nous parvient bleue et mourante à dessein,

—hardly an eighteenth-century sentiment. And "Les Ingénus" has an accent unknown to the world of La Pompadour, or, for that matter, to any world whatsoever before Verlaine: "Evening was falling, a dubious autumn evening; the fair ones hanging dreaming on our arms spoke such strange words in low tones that our soul ever since has been trembling and astonished":

Le soir tombait, un soir équivoque d'automne:
Les belles, se pendant rêveuses à nos bras,
Dirent alors des mots si spécieux, tout bas,
Que notre âme, depuis ce temps, tremble et s'étonne.

"Mandoline" is a fantasy in pastel shades: "Their short vests of silk, their long dresses with trains, their elegance, their joy and their soft blue shadows, whirl in the ecstacy of a pink and grey moon, and the mandolin babbles in the shivers of the breeze":

Leurs courtes vestes de soie,
Leurs longues robes à queues,
Leur élégance, leur joie
Et leurs molles ombres bleues.

Tourbillonnent dans l'extase
D'une lune rose et grise,
Et la mandoline jase
Parmi les frissons de brise.

Other poems ("Cortège," "Lettre," "Les Coquillages," "En Patinant") are more definitely "in the period" than the others. "En Patinant" reads like a verse rendering of Lancret's canvas, "L'Hiver." The nineteenth century was fond of such pastiche, whether in painting, verse, or interior decoration, and Verlaine's poems fit the taste of his age. In some ways they are less reminscent of Watteau than of painters like Ernest Meissonier (1815-91), whose dislike of contemporary dress was so great that he usually depicted his models in period costume, doublets and trunk hose or knee breeches and powdered wigs. And the flea-markets of Paris are still full of clocks, sconces, inkwells, and candelabra manufactured in imitation of an earlier day and now sold by dealers as "style Louis XV" or "style Louis XVI" with no guarantee of authenticity. Similarly, we cannot vouch for the authenticity of *Fêtes galantes*, if an eighteenth-century authenticity is implied. And indeed it is a question whether Verlaine was much interested in reconstructing a vanished age. The last poems of the volume forego the eighteenth century completely. "Colloque sentimentale" takes up the theme of "Après trois ans" in *Poèmes saturniens;* removed from its context it hardly evokes a blasé eighteenth-century couple; there is no period flavor of any sort. The poem could be a record of a promenade at Lécluse with Elisa Dujardin during Paul's second visit, when he found that his cousin's love had somehow waned: "Do you remember our former ecstacy?—Why do you expect me to remember it?"

—Te souvient-il de notre extase ancienne?
—Pourquoi voulez-vous donc qu'il m'en souvienne?

The poem which precedes it, "En Sourdine," is even freer of rococo detail. Comedians, marquises, fountains, statuary, all dissolve; reality is transposed into crepuscular suggestion: "Half close your eyes, fold your arms on your breast, and from your sleeping heart banish forever all thought . . ."

Ferme tes yeux à demi,
Croise tes bras sur ton sein,
Et de ton coeur endormi
Chasse à jamais tout dessein . . .

There is something miraculous about verse of this quality, and while neither *Poèmes saturniens* nor *Fêtes galantes* received much critical acclaim, they proved that a lyric talent of the first order had appeared in France.

VI *Crisis. Mathilde Mauté*

To people who knew him during these years—even men who, like Lepelletier, appreciated his talent—there was something disquieting about Verlaine. On the surface his life was reassuring enough. He was a frequent guest at the receptions of Mme de Ricard (Louis-Xavier's mother) and Nina de Callias, a good-natured Bohemian hostess of the period. He had his job at the City Hall and the backing of parents who were known to be well-off. And, however mediocre the success of his books, he had demonstrated that he was something more than a clever young man who talked about poetry: he also wrote it. But this façade concealed a permanent state of moral turmoil. His drinking, especially, had reached alarming proportions. Even his friends had to be careful. As in the case of his ancestors, alcohol unleashed some very unpleasant qualities. He was liable to fits of nearly homicidal rage, as when, walking one night with Lepelletier in the Bois, he attacked him with a sword stick.[25] All these excesses were efforts to dull something in himself. The question is—what?

There are a few clues to help us, and they fit what we know of Verlaine's personality. During the summer holidays in 1862 at Elisa Dujardin's house—the period when he first began drinking seriously—he met a boy of his own age who had become her cousin through marriage. "He wrote me about him in September and October, 1862, with enthusiasm," Lepelletier says, "just like a lover boasting about a mistress."[26] We cannot know what the nature of this relationship was: Lepelletier did not keep the letters, and Verlaine never alluded to the matter again. But one thing is strange: while he sighed with unrequited passion for Mme Dujardin (if passion it was), he was writing inflamed descriptions of a boy of eighteen. Do the tortured accents of "A une femme" and "L'Angoisse" in *Poèmes saturniens* refer to this situation (even though the verse was composed two or three years later) and indicate a sudden awareness of just how serious his problems were? Few homosexuals reach self-knowledge in a single flash of illumination. Understanding dawns slowly, through friendships growing warmer and more possessive, inexplicable jealousies, sudden tempests of emotion out of all proportion to the cause. The Lécluse visits may have been just such a stage in Verlaine's development. Nor was Elisa's cousin the only figure of this sort: ever since graduation, Paul had been seeing more and more of Lucien Viotti. As the 1860's passed, the relationship became more complicated and more intense. Here again, we cannot know how far things went. But the possibility that Lucien was a self-conscious invert who returned and even encouraged Verlaine's affection is very probable, as the end of the affair suggests.

This interpretation of the facts, I need hardly say, is purely theoretical. But it does help explain Verlaine's behavior at this moment—neurotic drinking, bouts of violence, and, finally, the incredible step of marriage. That the man who later decamped with Rimbaud, squandered a fortune on Létinois, made a fool of himself over Cazals, and crowned the whole by writing *Hombres* (one of the most detailed avowals of homosexuality ever penned) should have contemplated matrimony at all is extraordinary—all the more so when the lady involved was Mathilde Mauté de Fleurville, a typical *ingénue,* a veritable symbol of bourgeois respectability. Unless, indeed, these very qualities were the attraction. Until then he had sought nothing but coarse strumpets. Did he think that a complete change (which included dropping all interest in his own sex as well) would produce the cure he wanted? The increasing violence of his homosexual feelings showed him that inverted desire was something more than adolescent habit. It was growing stronger with time; he was torn between extremes and no sort of adjustment seemed possible.

Even nowadays the situation is difficult, and it was much worse a hundred years ago. None of the great manuals on sexual deviation had yet been published. Pederasty was of course known to exist; on occasion it was even widely discussed. But aside from undercover works like the Marquis de Sade's novels, it seldom appeared in print, and even the most daring writers were loath to mention it. Stendhal noted that a character in *Lucien Leuwen* was a homosexual, "but," he added, "you can't say so"—*cela ne peut se dire.* That was in 1834, and fifty years later even Zola, seldom afraid of the scabrous, gave up the idea of making one of his Rougon-Macquarts a deviant.[27] Gautier alone had dared a justification of pederasty, but in semicomic form, rather like *Charlie's Aunt:* the "man" d'Albert loves in *Mademoiselle de Maupin* turns out to be a woman in disguise. Lesbianism, it is true, had long enjoyed *droit de cité*—less, however, as a sexual anomaly than as an excuse for displays of female nudity. The nineteenth century's erotic symbol was Woman in her most generous and bosomy aspect, and Sapphic love doubled her seductions by adding a mate of her own sex. The true nature of Lesbianism—the masculine character of one of the partners—was not always understood. Baudelaire (in "Femmes damnées") noted this side of the question, but Baudelaire was always an exception and a precursor, here as elsewhere.[28] For the nineteenth-cenutry libertine, Lesbianism was *une touffe échevelée de baisers,* a disheveled tuft of kisses, as Mallarmé described it in *L'Après-midi d'un faune,* with an implied male figure grinning lecherously in the background. On the whole, this is the tone of Verlaine's six sonnets, *Les Amies,* which he published shortly after *Fêtes galantes.* His purpose is not altogether clear: Was he giving a demonstration of his talents as an erotic poet? Or expressing his own sexual dilemma in the only way then possible? Other poems he wrote at this time are perhaps less ambiguous: particularly "Le Monstre," an account of a nightmare which has been interpreted in Freudian terms as a symbolic confession of the two sources of his unrest—alcoholism and homosexuality.[29]

If such is really its significance, then he was a very distraught man; and marriage, hedged about with social and moral guarantees, appeared a solution to every difficulty. He did not understand (another characteristic of the bisexual) that the cure was worse than the disease: by satisfying one desire he gave fresh vigor to the other. Besides all this, his decision to marry was tantamount to sacrificing Lucien Viotti. The young man was deeply wounded, even desperate. On receiving the news he joined the army and was killed during the siege of Paris in 1871. Verlaine later hinted that Lucien had been secretly in love with Mathilde and that his death in battle was a kind of suicide.[30] This was cheap melodrama. He came nearer to confessing the truth in "A la Mémoire de mon ami Lucien Viotti," a prose-poem written in 1886, evoking his dead friend in tones of poignant regret: "I recall your dear presence. . . . Your eyes shine softly at me as of old, your voice reaches me deep and muted like the voice of former days. And your whole exquisite being of twenty, your charming head (like a handsomer Marceau's), the fine proportions of your ephebe's body . . . appear to me through my slowly falling tears. . . . Idiot that I was not to have understood in time!"[31] The lines imply that Lucien made advances which Verlaine did not take up. Given the poet's inflammable temperament, this is not altogether convincing; but however far their relations went, there was certainly a deep attraction, and it left Verlaine with a sinking-fund of remorse.

Mathilde Mauté de Fleurville was Charles de Sivry's half-sister. Verlaine met her at his friend's house one evening in June, 1869, and fell in love at once. A letter he wrote to a friend shows how he felt and explains the tone of *La Bonne Chanson,* the poems he began composing in Mathilde's honor almost at once: "A new, idyllic, florianesque Paul Verlaine . . . that's what I'm going to tell you about. . . . Through what miracle?—Look for the woman (I mean the *woman* of my dreams, the *wife* . . .) Who? you ask. Inquisitive man!—All I shall tell you is that She is charming, dainty, witty, that she likes poetry and corresponds point by point with my ideal. . . . We are not yet to the point of writing letters to each other, but every day, or almost, an artless poem comes from my calmed head and flies to her. People close to her tell me I need not despair, inasmuch as she doesn't exactly *hate* me; they even encourage my flirtation. If I'm still anxious and sad, it's delightfully so. You'll easily understand that in a charming situation like this I've renounced all drunkenness and all thought of a phallic trip to Arras: I want to deserve her!"[32] The truth was, he had just had his "phallic trip": he proposed marriage after a prolonged orgy of alcohol, sex, and self-doubt in an Arras brothel.

But his enthusiasm, as far as it went, was genuine enough. Mathilde was fresh, pretty, well-bred, and elegant; she even wrote verse herself and had read *Poèmes saturniens* and *Fêtes galantes.* And—what Verlaine does not say (perhaps he did not consciously realize that it was the greatest attraction of all)—she was only sixteen. To a debauchee like him, a young girl of good family, a virgin, had all the piquancy of the unknown. Salacious minds are always titillated by innocence. Hence the reasons for the marriage and the explanation of its subsequent collapse. As far as Verlaine was concerned, it was not based on genuine esteem and affection but on pure libidinousness: a lust bound to flag in the long run since innocence cannot be enjoyed without ceasing to be innocent. Mathilde's novelty would vanish with the wedding night; she fulfilled a momentary need only. Verlaine was tired of promiscuity (or thought he was) and frightened by tendencies he dared not avow. In his own words, as he recalled the situation twenty-five years afterwards, he "wanted to change his life,"[33] wanted a home (the childhood fixation again) and the peace and security home brings. And so he fell in love. Had there been anyone to consult, anyone who could have advised him, things might have been different; but his father had died on December 30, 1865, leaving nobody but an adoring mother whose only thought was to satisfy her son's whims—marriage included, if that was what he demanded.

Mathilde was not unattracted. He was a poet, a man with a future; she saw herself inspiring his work, sharing his glory, presiding over artistic little teas. True, he was not handsome,[34] but she did not find him as ugly as most people thought: "While he talked to me his glance, usually black and gleaming, became coaxing and gentle; he smiled. . . . At that moment he wasn't ugly."[35] On the whole, her mother agreed with her. M. Mauté, a retired notary with nobiliary pretensions (the "de Fleurville" in the name was a status symbol, and corresponded to nothing real), had some misgivings; but he ended by consenting—for reasons which are not far to seek. Elisa Verlaine proved unexpectedly rich: she guaranteed her son 60,000 francs as a marriage settlement and declared that since Paul was in love he would ask no dowry in return. These were cogent arguments. Mauté had another daughter as well, and a dowry was important in nineteenth-century France; more than one promising union never took place through lack of it. Mathilde, in her *Mémoires*, tries to paint her father as a wealthy man, a sort of landed aristocrat (she had a streak of snobbery in her nature: it was the worst failing of an otherwise decent woman); but everything suggests that his resources were very limited. Like many others he was keeping up a front: a country estate, a house in town; he needed every franc of ready cash. Verlaine's proposal was both honorable and advantageous; it settled a problem that must have worried Mauté more than once. The wedding took place the following year, August 11, 1870.

VI La Bonne Chanson *and After*

During the intervening months Verlaine wrote a series of poems to Mathilde completed in 1871 as *La Bonne Chanson*. They are disappointing by comparison with *Poèmes saturniens* and *Fêtes galantes*. He was trying to be respectable, and the role did not suit him. In Mathilde he saw a refuge from himself, or part of himself; and it was the part that represented his true genius: restlessness, searching, intense sensation, sexual ambiguity, moral crisis. Hence the relative mediocrity of the new book. "Away with abominable hatreds! Away with the forgetfulness sought in abhorrèd drinks! . . . Guided by you, beautiful eyes with tender flames, I want to walk, yes, calm and upright throughout life. . . . Without violence, regret or desire. . . . And truly I seek no other Paradise":

> Arrière la rancune abominable! arrière
> L'oubli qu'on cherche en des breuvages exécrés! . . .
> Je veux, guidé par vous, beaux yeux aux flammes douces . . .
> Oui, je veux marcher droit et calme dans la Vie . . .
> Sans violence, sans remords et sans envie . . .
> Et vraiment je ne veux pas d'autre Paradis.

No writer ever renounced his talent more completely: had Mathilde really been the paradise he sought, his poetic career would have been over. "We shall walk, hand in hand, at the same pace, blessed with the childlike souls of those who love purely, shan't we?"

> . . . Nous marcherons pourtant du même pas,
> Et la main dans la main, avec l'âme enfantine
> De ceux qui s'aiment sans mélange, n'est-ce pas?

Only one or two poems match the quality of his first volumes, "Avant que tu ne t'en ailles," a beautiful love lyric, and "La lune blanche,' where we find once more the style and accent of "Mon Rêve familier" and "En Sourdine": "The white moon shines in the woods; from each branch a voice is heard beneath the trees. . . . Oh, well-beloved."

> La lune blanche
> Luit dans les bois;
> De chaque branche
> Part une voix
> Sous la ramée . . .
> O bien aimée.

Were it not for these, *La Bonne Chanson* would be a failure.

And there was worse to follow; not what he wrote but what he did not write. For the next eighteen months he wrote nothing at all. As long as his marriage lasted he was mute. Fortunately, it did not last very long.

Difficulties began within less than six months. The young couple had found an apartment at 2 rue du Cardinal-Lemoine; and by the time they were settled, the Franco-Prussian War (which broke out on July 19, 1870) had reached a disastrous stage. Napoleon III's armies were defeated at Sedan and Paris under siege. Mathilde was sincerely in love with her husband, and she met the situation as best she could. Tried to be sprightly, struggled in the kitchen with horse meat and rat. It was all in vain. Verlaine found the meals impossible, and as far as marriage went the novelty had worn off. He had had his wedding night. Mathilde was no longer a virgin; she was, indeed, soon pregnant. And with his exquisite poetic sense he had no difficulty in perceiving that her interest in literature was so much idle chatter; she could not tell good verse from bad. And she was a check on his liberty. He had to come home at regular hours, account for his movements, make conversation with a woman who bored him more and more. Perhaps for this reason he joined the National Guard: it gave him an excuse for absenting himself as much as he liked. Guard duty included drinks. Before long he was coming home drunk; he was even casting an eye on the housemaid. When Mathilde protested (about the drinking—she did not find out about the maid until 1894, when she read her ex-husband's *Confessions*) the arguments got high. Before long they ended in blows.

Meanwhile, Paris had refused to ratify the truce Adolphe Thiers negotiated with the victorious Prussians. An extreme leftist group known as the Commune seized control of the city; Verlaine joined the insurgents and was given a post as newspaper censor. Thiers and his government fled to Versailles and set about retaking the capital, street by street. There followed one of the most brutal episodes in French history. After several weeks of savage combat, the Versailles troops had the mastery and a severe repression followed: anonymous denunciations, mass arrests, summary courts-martial. Verlaine was panic-stricken: his association with the Commune automatically made him a suspect. He packed up and fled with Mathilde to his mother's relatives at Fampoux

(June, 1871). The summer passed and by September the worst was over. But even when he ventured back to Paris, he avoided the rue du Cardinal-Lemoine. He settled with Mathilde's parents, who had a house in the rue Nicolet (Montmartre), and made no attempt to return to the City Hall. He was convinced that his adhesion to the Commune had cost him his position; but in any case office routine had long bored him and he was glad of an excuse to drop it. It was at this moment—jobless, drinking again, tired of Mathilde and, perhaps, regretting Lucien Viotti—that he received the two letters from Arthur Rimbaud.

CHAPTER 2

Rimbaud: Achievement and Disaster

I *Adolescent Genius*

HE said he was eighteen, that he wanted to write a long poem and could not do it at Charleville: his mother, a devout widow, kept him short of money, so short that he did not even have the fare to Paris. To prove that his pretensions were genuine he enclosed some manuscript poems: "Les Effarés," "Accroupissements," "Les Douaniers," "Le Coeur volé." Verlaine read them with amazement, showed them to some of his friends. Their opinion was unanimous: the verse had genius (a judgment posterity has confirmed). He sent Rimbaud an enthusiastic reply, with money enclosed for a train ticket, and the boy arrived in Paris a few days later, September 10, 1871.

Nobody could have been better suited to overwhelm Verlaine. Born October 20, 1854, Rimbaud was not yet seventeen: he had added eighteen months to his age to make his talent seem more plausible. He had beauty—the fair-haired, blue-eyed sort that is often the most seductive of all—and he was even more savage and iconoclastic than most brilliant young men. Modern enthusiasm has somewhat exaggerated the originality of his ideas. Nothing he said was particularly new, but he said it more provocatively than anyone else and practiced it in his verse with a daring beyond any previous example. "The Poet makes himself a seer by a long, immense and logical disorder of all his senses. . . . He seeks out all forms of love, suffering, madness. . . . He becomes the great invalid, the great criminal, the great accursed —and the supreme Sage!—He achieves the *unknown!*" Only a few earlier writers, notably Baudelaire, found favor in his eyes, and then with reservations: "Baudelaire is the first seer, king of poets, *a true God.* But he lived in too artistic an environment, and the form so praised in his work is second-rate. The inventions of the unknown require new forms."[1] He had read *Poèmes saturniens* and *Fêtes galantes,* and there is reason to suppose that he had some inkling of their author's sexual tastes.[2] Thus equipped he was well able to detect not only the pose and artificiality of Parnassianism, but also the numbing platitude of Verlaine's life in the rue Nicolet and his secret discontent.

Confronted with this phenomenon, the older poet was defenseless. The slumbering homosexuality of his nature awakened all the keener after two years' abstinence. In the light of the new revelation, Mathilde's shortcomings were brutally apparent. She was conventional, stupid, and a drag upon him; she had saddled him with her family (it never occurred to him that he had been as anxious to move in with the Mautés as she), and she was eight months' pregnant. And now here was a tempestuous youth offering pleasure and adventure, both sensuous and intellectual, beyond anything he had ever known. Incapable of restraint or self-discipline he yielded to the temptation at once. His marriage had been shaky enough before Rimbaud arrived; it now collapsed utterly and with it all the social and moral guarantees it had provided.

There has been some debate as to which partner played the decisive role, and seduced the other.[3] Verlaine, with ten years' seniority, would seem the likeliest candidate; but on the other hand he was timid and easily led, with none of Rimbaud's violence. The point is not of much importance. Whichever took the first step the other followed willingly: Verlaine had desire, knowledge, and experience, and Rimbaud a theoretical intransigence that stopped at nothing. All spiritual chains were bad, he held; and woman, representing marriage and the family, was the worst of all: "I don't like women," he wrote shortly afterwards. "Love must be reinvented. Women are interested in nothing but an assured social position, and once they have it they discard all thought of sentiment and beauty. Nothing remains but cold disdain, the food of marriage nowadays."[4] For the first time Verlaine heard a justification of desires he had scarcely dared admit even to himself: he was later to develop the theme in poems like "Ces passions" of *Parallèlement.* Rimbaud dragged into the light and exalted tendencies until then clandestine and unavowed; he had an adolescent craving for new experience, precisely because it was new. We know nothing of his sexual habits before he left Charleville: whatever has been written on the subject is idle speculation. A school friend, Ernest Delahaye, saw nothing unusual in this side of his life—but then neither did Lepelletier in Verlaine's. Both biographers lacked penetration and were inclined to count too much on boyhood intimacy. It is not true that an adolescent has no secrets from friends of his own age. He often has a great many. Even as children individuals like Rimbaud and Verlaine frequently divide their lives into compartments. Delahaye was an intelligent chum with whom Rimbaud could discuss literature, but there may have been another side of his life which he did not discuss at all. The main quality Delahaye remembered was the boy's charm, "both moral and physical"; and the description he has left of it helps explain Rimbaud's impact on Verlaine: "His features were not handsome in the ordinary sense . . . but they had a rugged, healthy simplicity: thick lips . . . a slim nose, large, broad forehead . . . pink cheeks firmly modelled, eyes of a profound, limpid blue—delightful eyes, terrifying almost in their mixture of innocence and pitiless lucidity! . . . When one knew him, one felt oneself the intimate of a king, a hero, a magician and a saint. One felt penetrated with luminous rays, as it were; protected, uplifted by an invincible force; one experienced security, pride, and a species of happiness impossible to describe."[5]

The course of events once this prodigy got to the rue Nicolet was rapid and destructive. He took an immediate dislike to Mathilde, and the feeling was wholly mutual. His manners were deliberately outrageous. This was partly a defense mechanism, he knew he was a boor, and, reared in strict and almost peasant frugality, he could not adapt himself to the bourgeois refinements of the Mauté household. They filled him with uneasiness which he concealed behind a mask of contempt. He even exaggerated his coarseness: ate like a hog at table, smoked a foul-smelling pipe, filled his bed with lice, and stole anything that took his fancy (a bit of antique ivory, one of M. Mauté's hunting knives). Within two weeks Mathilde and her mother had had enough (Mauté was absent in the country), and they insisted that he leave. Verlaine lodged him with various friends. They tried to be kind, but the results were always the same. Rimbaud was so gracelessly obstreperous that one after another they lost patience and turned him out. In the end, Verlaine found an attic for him in the rue Campagne-Première.

We get an idea of the sort of impression he made from a passage in Lepelletier's book: "To please Verlaine, I invited Rimbaud to my house for dinner. . . . He refused to say a word during the first part of the meal, only opening his mouth to drink or to ask for bread, and then in sharp, brief tones as though he were in a restaurant. Afterwards, under the influence of some strong Burgundy, with which Verlaine plied him generously, he became aggressive—giving vent to irritating paradoxes and maxims designed to provoke contradiction. He attacked me especially as a 'saluter of the dead' because he had seen me take off my hat when a funeral passed. I had just lost my mother, and I quickly silenced him on this point, looking at him in a manner that made him furious. He got up and came towards me menacingly. In a nervous and silly way he'd grabbed up a dessert-knife from the table. I pinned his hand against his shoulder and made him sit down again at once. . . . Verlaine interposed, begged me not to be angry, and excused his friend."[6]

His behavior in literary circles was not better. He was introduced to the Parnassians, some of whom, like Albert Mérat, had seen his verse and admired it. But Rimbaud did not admire theirs and said so in obscene terms. In the end, poets and writers refused to have him at their meetings: if Verlaine wanted to come, he was welcome; but he must come alone. He was offended, and a breach opened between him and his old friends (all except Lepelletier) which grew wider week by week and was never afterwards totally closed. Within a short time he was ostracized with Rimbaud, in a frenzied world of their own, where drink, sex, and poetry—"a long, immense and logical disorder of all the senses"—were all that counted. They began frequenting the most extreme groups of the contemporary Bohemia. Besides liquor, Rimbaud experimented with hashish, then as now a favorite diversion in offbeat circles. Despite his marriage, Verlaine had never lost touch with certain friends whose tastes were known to be sexually unorthodox. One of them, E. Cabaner, was much taken with Rimbaud, lodged him for a while, began to think of him as a permanent companion, a characteristic homosexual dream: "I would give you food, clothes, a bed if you wished," he wrote in an elegy. "Yes, I'd be more than a mother to you; because for many years, seeking a friend on this earth, I've been waiting, waiting, waiting!"

> Mais je t'offrirais: nourriture,
> Vêtements, . . . lit, si tu voulais.
> Oui, je serais plus qu'une mère
> Pour toi, car depuis longtemps,
>
> Cherchant un ami sur la terre,
> J'attends, j'attends, j'attends! . . .[7]

This warm admiration was perhaps one reason why Verlaine found the room in the rue Campagne-Première: he had no intention of being supplanted by Cabaner. Before 1871 was over, he was parading his new passion with strange lack of reticence. Much ill-natured gossip began: the two friends were soon known throughout the Latin Quarter as practicing inverts.

In retrospect we can see that Rimbaud meant something more to Verlaine than mere amorous adventure. Paul was born to live outside and beyond normal experience, and his homosexual instincts were linked to whatever was most original in his talent. When he denied them by marriage, inspiration dried up. His genius could not function within any set of rules, much less the humdrum rules of conjugality. Ever since *La Bonne Chanson* (which, for that matter, was a song of anticipation, not fulfillment) he had stopped writing, and the first poems of *Romances sans paroles* began to appear within a few months of Rimbaud's arrival.[8] Had the young genius not erupted onto the stifling scene of the rue Nicolet, Verlaine would almost certainly have petered out in dullness and sterility; have remained, as Delahaye puts it, "the delicate, subtle Parisian, affecting airs of elegant boredom, frittering away his life in the ultra-refinement of literary circles."[9]

But the freedom Rimbaud gave had to be paid for, and, if literature gained, everything else suffered. Besides losing his friends, Verlaine was also losing his wife. She has described his behavior at this moment: he was constantly drunk; the sentimental world of *La Bonne Chanson* degenerated into a nightmare of curses and physical violence, which spared neither Mathilde nor her infant son (Georges Verlaine was born on October 30, 1871). There is no reason to question the details:

they correspond point by point with what others have written of Verlaine in his cups. Lepelletier's testimony (and he was a friend and admirer) is just as unfavorable: "Sober, Verlaine was the gentlest, most agreeable of companions, and doubtless of husbands; but intoxicated with absinth, curaçao, gin or American grog, he became, even for his best friends, aggressive, violent, in a word unbearable. If he was like this with us, in cafés, it is not hard to imagine his conduct when he returned home, often very late, following a few last solitary drinks after he'd left us."[10] Mathilde tried to conceal what was going on: she loved him and there was also her pride: "I was so ashamed, so humiliated at having married a drunk, that I preferred to put up with anything rather than admit the truth to my family."[11] But when Verlaine one night tried to strangle her and was only prevented from doing so by Mauté himself, the whole story came out: the increasing brutality, the insane rages. Next day she left Paris with her father and refused to come back until Verlaine had severed all connection with Rimbaud. It was a strange ultimatum, and the very fact that it could be made, that a wife could threaten to leave her husband unless he gave up an adolescent friend of his own sex, shows how badly things had gone in the home. Yet it is a question whether Mathilde and her father understood all Rimbaud's significance. They thought of him chiefly as a bad influence: "Rimbaud, who was quite worthless, got Verlaine drinking absinth, which unchained his worst instincts."[12] (The accusation was not entirely just; Verlaine had had a taste for absinth long before he met Rimbaud.) They never seem to have asked themselves what sort of influence it was that could enable a boy of eighteen to dominate a man of twenty-eight to such a point that his wife was reduced to living in terror of her life.

M. Mauté's chief purpose, indeed, was to re-establish the marriage: when Verlaine refused to drop Rimbaud, steps were initiated to obtain a legal separation—a heavy threat, but with no end in view than recapturing the erring husband. Verlaine had to yield, Mathilde had the law on her side: there had been marks on her neck after the strangulation attempt—Mauté had had them duly attested by a physician. Rimbaud was sent back to Charleville. But once Mathilde had regained the rue Nicolet, he returned to Paris (May 18), exasperated by her brief victory. To make sure that his hold over Verlaine would henceforth be complete, he persuaded him to desert his family and leave for Brussels—July 7, 1872.

III *Belgium and England*

The flight was prepared in secrecy and executed without warning. Elisa Verlaine had always been too fond of her son to like his wife much, and she produced what money was necessary. "She consented to Paul's departure and even supplied the cash—an unfortunate encouragement since without it Verlaine could not have begun the vagabond existence which was to end so disastrously."[13] For nearly a fortnight Mathilde did not even know what had become of her husband. He finally wrote from Brussels. The letter was a curious illustration of his self-contradictory nature: "My poor Mathilde, don't grieve, don't cry; I'm living a bad dream; I'll come back one day."[14] When he was with his wife he wanted Rimbaud; and now that he had Rimbaud he regretted Mathilde. The Mautés discussed the situation and finally decided that Mathilde, chaperoned by her mother, should go to Belgium and persuade Verlaine to come home. Her attempt nearly succeeded. They met in a Brussels hotel and after a passionate interview during which she played the trump card of sex for all it was worth, she got him onto the train. It looked as though she had won. But Verlaine had only yielded to a stronger will. Resistance, the resistance of the weak, was building up within him: apprehension of the old life in the rue Nicolet, thoughts of Rimbaud, deserted and penniless in a foreign town. When the passengers disembarked at the border for the customs examination, Mathilde lost sight of her husband, and the train was already in motion again when she noticed him standing on the platform. Despite her appeals, he refused to get on; they never met again.

She reached Paris completely discouraged and next day received a brief and obscene note (written, apparently, while her husband waited for a train back to Brussels), informing her that she was a "louse," fit to be squashed and dropped into a chamber pot, and that he was returning to Rimbaud, "whose heart she had nearly broken," provided the boy would forgive him "for what she'd made him do."[15] Backed by her father and the family lawyer, she applied for legal separation (divorce did not exist in France until 1885), producing as evidence all Rimbaud's letters to her husband which Verlaine, careless as ever, had left behind in a desk. Just what they contained cannot now be known; Mathilde later burned the entire collection. But the court had no doubts: "the correspondence proves that Verlaine was carrying on infamous relations with a young man."[16] Together with the charge of desertion, this was considered more than sufficient to justify a separation, granted on October 13, with custody of Georges and 1200 francs a year alimony.

For the next eighteen months Verlaine and Rimbaud were vagabonds, freed from all restraint: "He'd left a number of mortified fools behind in Paris," Verlaine wrote later, "and I a certain Princess Bitch":

> Lui quelques sots bernés, et moi
> Certaine princesse Souris.

They were indifferent to everything but themselves. A police report of August 1, 1873, says, "in Brussels, the two friends were seen to practice their love openly."[17] The situation, however, was not nearly so smooth as it appeared. Rimbaud's account in *Une Saison en Enfer* is as near the truth as any we have, and it shows that relations soon proved unsatisfactory. The two poets were totally unlike: Verlaine was emotional and sensitive, seeking protection and reassurance: "This evening I leaned over you as you slept," he wrote in a sonnet, "Life, what a delicate marvel it is—since our whole being is nought but a wilting flower":

> Ce soir, je m'étais penché sur ton sommeil . . .
> Qu'on vive, ô quelle délicate merveille,
> Tant notre appareil est une fleur qui plie! . . .[18]

Rimbaud found this sort of thing a nuisance: it was disgustingly sentimental and it kept him awake: "Almost every night, as soon as I'd fallen asleep, the wretched brother would get up . . . and drag me out of bed, shrieking his idiot's regrets." The idiot's regrets were the most exasperating detail of all—regrets for the lost domesticity of the rue Nicolet. In Rimbaud's view he had rendered Verlaine a positive service by getting him out of that private little quagmire: "I'd indeed undertaken to give him back his primitive state of a son of the Sun." He saw their relationship as a new experience, a search for liberty and the creation of fresh poetic forms. Travel fitted the same pattern. He made no secret of his intention to desert his companion one day for new pastures: "After a penetrating caress, he said: 'One day I must go away, very far. . . .' "[19] His relationship with Verlaine was the union of a sentimental libertine and a ruthless intellectual; inevitably it could not last. The love sessions grew rarer, the stormy scenes more and more frequent. In the end (as Verlaine said) their life together became one long scene.[20]

They went to London together on September 7, 1872. The change of scenery did little to improve their friendship, but it brought out an unexpected talent in Verlaine. His sketches of the English capital in his letters to Lepelletier are graphic and lively; it is strange that they are not better known. What an Englishman would have taken as a matter of course he found startlingly novel:

"Flat as a black bug—that's London! Small black houses, or huge 'Gothic' and 'Venetian' buildings like side-boards. . . . Four or five cafés where you can get something drinkable . . . the others are dining rooms, where alcohol is not served, or coffee-houses from which spirits are carefully banished. 'We have no spirits,' a maid replied when I asked her the insidious question 'one absinth, if you please, Mademoisell! . . . A crowd of boys in red shines your boots from morning to evening for a penny. . . . In the theatres (what a smell of feet!) the actresses are so thin they make you weep. . . . At the music halls (Alhambra, Grecian Theatre, etc.) a jig is danced between two renderings of *God Save the Queen*. . . . The Thames is superb: imagine a huge whirlpool of mud: something like an overflowing latrine. Babylonian bridges with hundreds of cast-iron pillars thick and high as the Vendôme column, painted blood red. . . . Thanks to the incredible traffic of carriages, cabs, omnibuses (filthy, by the way), the tramways, the railroads eternally thundering over splendid metal bridges, and the incredibly brutal pedestrians, the aspect of the streets is, if not Parisian, at least very entertaining. . . . to sum up: it's all very unexpected, and a hundred times more *amusing* than Italy, Spain and the shores of the Rhine."—"London is less gloomy than its reputation: I find many distractions here. But as for clean cafés—nix! nix! You've got to get used to the filthy pot-houses called *French Coffee houses* or the travelling-salesman dives in Leicester Square. However! This incredible town is not bad—raven-black and noisy; prudish—and with *every vice wide open;* eternally drunk, despite the ridiculous parliamentary 'bills' on drunkenness; immense, although at bottom it is nothing but a collection of small towns—back-biting, jealous, ugly, and flat; quite without public buildings, except for its interminable docks (which are sufficient as far as my poetic ideas, more and more *modern,* go) . . ."—"The fog is beginning to show the end of its dirty nose. Everybody's coughing—except me. . . . As for the women: incredible hair-dos, velvet bracelets with steel buckles, red shawls. . . . all pretty with a nasty expresssion and 'angelic' voices . . . exquisite *misses* in long red satin skirts—mud-splashed, drink-stained and holed with cigarette burns—Negroes everywhere: in the streets and music-halls, where they make excellent clowns. They're an import from America."—"I've seen *Macbeth.* The orchestra started things off with the ouverture from *La Dame Blanche,* and played quadrilles by Métra during the intermissions. The sets were very pretty. This was at the Princess Theatre."—"The City is really an interesting section: incredible activity is narrow, black streets bordered by handsome buildings—offices, banks, warehouses, etc. I went the other day by boat as far as Woolwich: the docks are amazing: Carthage! Tyre!"

"The London Sunday: at 1:00, everything is closed—everything! From one to three, a few rare public-houses and dining rooms set their doors ajar under the eye of a policeman who, watch in hand, supervises the opening and closing. From six to eleven, the same thing. Aside from these establishments, everything shuts down—even the independent shoe-shiners. One of them, as he did my boots last Sunday, was sharply reprimanded by a passing constable. I said 'independent shoe-shiners,' for the boys in red I've already mentioned are managed by a charity organization which, of course, makes them pass the Lord's Day adoring the Lord. Mail, railways (during the hour of religious services), shipping, all public services are dead,—except for telegraph and boats on the Thames. In parentheses: you can drink on those boats—outside the legal hours: how many drunks go through London on Sundays, from Woolwich to Battersea! . . . Of course there's no theatre. Preaching and hymn-singing in the open air."—"In all London there are only six urinals. It's true that each one of those interesting structures is papered with small yellow advertisements, stating that William George, of Castle Street, has a large and varied assortment of 'French letters'.—Coffee, which is atrocious, costs six-pence, without brandy. The fish is dreadful: sole, mackerel, whiting like so much squid, soft, sticky, runny . . . Luke-warm beer . . . The English bars are worth a description. The outsides are in mahogany-finished wood, with heavy copper embellishments. Up to a man's height the windows are glazed, with flowers, birds, etc. polished in the glass. You enter through a terribly thick door, held half-open by a formidable strap which (I mean the door) smaçks your buttocks after first knocking off your hat. The inside is very confined: a mahogany bar with zinc top along which, either standing or perched on high narrow stools, are well-dressed men, sordid beggars, street-porters in white, fat cab-drivers, all drinking, smoking, and talking through their noses. Behind the counter serve bar-keeps with their sleeves rolled up or girls, usually pretty, slightly dishevelled, elegantly dressed in bad taste, whom you poke with your hand, your cane or your umbrella, to an accompaniment of loud laughs and off-colour remarks which don't seem to offend them much. . . . English toilets have been overpraised: the water comes into the bowls with such violence that the 'visitor' is splashed all over. . . . Toilets in cafés are called *lavatories* because they include taps, wash-basins, soap, etc. When you come out, you fall into the hands of boys who, for tuppence, brush you off from head to toe: I don't know what else they'd be willing to do for a little more money—"

"There's an unknown curiosity here—the Tower Subway—a tube fifty metres long under the Thames. You go down into it by a hundred steps or so. It is *literally* a metal tube with gas-jets at head-level and a walk about half a metre wide. It stinks, it's warm, and it vibrates like a suspension bridge—all to the uproar of the surrounding water. I'm very glad I saw it. But when you reflect that it was built with all the temerity of the English and carelessness of danger those strange people show, you feel a delicious, cowardly shudder as you emerge."—"Here I am, you'll say, sunk in Anglicism . . . I think I told you in one of my last letters that I was looking for whatever was *good* here. Well, I think I've found it: something very gentle, almost childish, very young, very candid with at the same time certain amusing and charming brutalities and gaieties. To find it you have delve deep, get over many prejudices, many habits—and doubtless these people are not as good as we are—they are less *good* in the sense that they are too chauvinistic, and their souls, hearts and minds are despairingly *special*. But that very *specialty* is exquisite, and there's a good deal of simplicity even in their species of egotism. Even their ridiculous characteristics are by no means odious."—"The Grenadiers (splendid men in red, curled and pomaded) 'give their arm' to ladies every Sunday for sixpence. But the Horse Guards, dressed in breastplates, high boots, helmets with white plumes, charge a shilling!"—"Yesterday was Christmas! A worse sort of Sunday, because so cursedly pious! But *l'oie*—the Goose—is exquisite. I stuffed myself on it at the houses of some of the natives, *with apple sauce!*"[21]

The "modernism" of some of these details is interesting, corresponding as it does with similar themes Verlaine admired in Baudelaire. We see its influence in *Romances sans paroles* and still later in volumes like *Sagesse* and *Amour*. Before he could make much use of the idea, however, his relations with Rimbaud had reached breaking point.

On July 3, 1873, they were sharing a cheap room at 34-35 Howland Street, Fitzroy Square, and funds had run low. Verlaine went shopping and returned with a bottle of oil and a herring. The spectacle excited Rimbaud's verve: "What an ass you look with your bottle and your herring!" Verlaine revolted. A spoiled child, as he grows up, may nourish a sense of guilt and a desire for atonement; but when he atones he expects something in return. Unqualified brutality will not hold him forever. His weakness shows itself in contradictory ways: submission at one moment, resentment and flight the next. He is masochistic to a point, and after that he rebels. Verlaine had been sorely tried for months; and now that Mathilde had got her separation, he was beginning to realize what his crazy escapade would cost. He threw the herring at his friend. As Rimbaud watched, astounded, he stuffed clothes into a valise and rushed out to a wharf on the Thames where the Belgian steam-packet was taking on passengers. Arthur could not go aboard because he had no money: he was still on the pier making frantic signals as the ship cast off and disappeared down the river.[22]

IV Romances sans paroles

It was against this background that *Romances sans paroles*

was begun and completed. The earliest poems date from the spring of 1872, within six months of Rimbaud's arrival in Paris; the rest were composed during the following year, as we see from Verlaine's letters. "I have some very curious notes on Belgium," he wrote Blémont from London on September 22, 1872, enclosing several items from the new book. "My treasure has increased greatly during the fortnight I've been here." And on October 5, to the same friend: "My little volume is entitled *Romances sans paroles*. . . . The whole is a series of vague impressions, sad and gay, with a touch of almost naive picturesqueness—*Paysages belges,* for example." The completed manuscript was sent to Lepelletier on May 19, 1873: it was dedicated to Rimbaud: "You'll receive at the same time as this letter the famous manuscript . . . I attach great importance to the dedication. First of all *as a protest*"—the success of Mathilde's separation demand had further increased the gossip in literary circles, where the homosexual rumors were now taken as confirmed—"then because he was there when these poems were written and encouraged me to write them, and above all as a proof of gratitude for the devotion and affection he has always shown me, especially when I was sick and nearly died."[23] It was true that in December and January 1872-73, Verlaine had been seriously ill in London; but since Rimbaud was temporarily absent at Charleville, where he had gone the previous November, and did not return to England until Elisa Verlaine, at her son's request, sent him 50 francs for the trip, it is difficult to see how he can have played the devoted role Verlaine assigns him, the more so as Elisa herself remained until February, when the worst was over. Verlaine was doubtless doing his best to see Rimbaud as a tender and loving companion, no easy task; and he also wanted to furnish Lepelletier with some kind of explanation for his passionate interest in the boy.

The three sections of *Romances sans paroles (Ariettes oubliées, Paysages belges,* and *Aquarelles)* contain some of Verlaine's most beautiful verse, but beneath the exquisite surface the tone is restless and uneasy. If Rimbaud, as we might expect, is the chief inspiration, it is an inspiration which, besides not daring to name itself, is also troubled by regrets for Mathilde. The poems of *Ariettes oubliées* alternate between the friend and the wife, thus introducing the theme of sexual parallelism, which Verlaine was to treat more fully in *Parallèlement* seventeen years later. *Romances sans paroles,* however, has none of the explicit frankness of that volume: the poet was not yet ready to admit his homosexual tendencies, even to himself; he wrote in the style of "En sourdine" and "La lune blanche" of *Fêtes galantes* and *La Banne Chanson,* transferring to Rimbaud the music and phraseology he had already used to celebrate Elisa Dujardin and Mathilde Mauté: "It's the laguourous ecstacy, it's the amorous fatigue, it's all the rustle of the forest in the embrace of the breezes, and, in the grey branches, it's the choir of tiny voices. . . . that lamenting soul, and that sleeping complaint, is ours, isn't it? Mine, tell me, and yours, whose humble anthem swells in low tones through the warm evening?"

> C'est l'extase langoureuse,
> C'est la fatigue amoureuse,
> C'est tous les frissons des bois
> Parmi l'étreinte des brises,
> C'est, vers les ramures grises,
> Le choeur des petites voix . . .
> Cette âme qui se lamente
> Et cette plainte dormante
> C'est la nôtre, n'est-ce pas?
> La mienne, dis, et la tienne,
> Dont s'exhale l'humble antienne
> Par ce tiède soir, tout bas?

Such is the predominant tone of *Ariettes oubliés:* reality only impinges on the dream world in attenuated and plaintive form: "I guess, through a murmur, the subtle contour of old voices, and in the musical gleams, oh pale love, a future dawn!"

> Je devine, à travers un murmure,
> Le contour subtil des voix anciennes
> Et dans les lueurs musiciennes,
> Amour pâle, une aurore future!

There is a harmony of moods and echoes with no positive statement of any kind: "It weeps in my heart as it rains on the town. What is this languour that penetrates my heart? . . . It's indeed the worst suffering not to know why, without either love or hatred, my heart is so sad!"

Il pleure dans mon coeur
Comme il pleut sur la ville;
Quelle est cette langueur
Qui pénètre mon coeur? . . .
C'est bien la pire peine
De ne savoir pourquoi
Sans amour et sans haine
Mon coeur a tant de peine!

In verse of this kind the technical and stylistic experiments evident here and there in his earlier work reach perfection. *Romances sans paroles* is the first of his books which is entirely *his own,* with no trace of Hugo, Leconte de Lisle or Baudelaire. It is the culmination of the first part of his career, taking us to the brink of *Sagesse*, when he adopted other themes; and he continued to write in this style for another year, until well into 1874: certain poems composed in prison, like "Le ciel est par-dessus le toit" and "Art poétique" belong more properly to *Romances sans paroles* than to *Sagesse* and *Jadis et Naguère* in which (1880, 1888) they were eventually published.

The *Ariettes* are unquestionably the best of *Romances sans paroles*, although the other two sections contain much beautiful verse. *Paysages belges* evokes the travels with Rimbaud—the freedom of new sights and sounds. "Walcourt" catches the charm of a country town: its brick and tile, the surrounding vineyards, the wide roads with their promise of liberty, and the gay crowds of the inns. "Bricks and tiles, oh, charming little refuges for lovers!"

Briques et tuiles,
O les charmants
Petits asiles
Pour les amants!

"Charleroi" is an attempt to sketch an industrialized city: stations, railways, blast furnaces and the general atmosphere of sinister activity in which the inhabitants seem changed into malignant gnomes: "Brutal places! the stench of human sweat, the cries of metal! In the black grass the Kobolds pass . . .":

Sites brutaux!
Oh! votre haleine,
Sueur humaine,
Cris des métaux!
Dans l'herbe noire
Les Kobolds vont . . .

Verlaine was not very well suited to somber themes like these. He does better in "Bruxelles," subtitled "simple fresques," which is roughly an approximation of Impressionist painting: "The flight of hills and ramps is greenish and pink in the half-light of the lamps where everything is confused. . . . The chateau is white, with, on its side, the setting sun":

La fuite est verdâtre et rose
Des collines et des rampes
Dans un demi-jour de lampes
Qui vient brouiller toute chose . . .

Le château, tout blanc
Avec, à son flanc,
Le soleil couché . . .

Perhaps the most successful of all—less impressionistic and more "Verlainian"—is "Chevaux de bois," a description of a merry-go-round seen in a street fair: "Turn, turn, good wooden horses, turn a hundred times, turn a thousand times, turn often and keep on turning, turn, turn to the sound of the oboes. . . . Keep on turning without any need of spurs to make you continue your circular gallop, and keep on turning without hope of fodder":

Tournez, tournez, bons chevaux de bois,
Tournez cent tours, tournez mille tours,
Tournez souvent et tournez toujours,
Tournez, tournez au son des hautbois . . .
Tournez, tournez, sans qu'il soit besoin
D'user jamais de nuls éperons
Pour commander à vos galops ronds,
Tournez, tournez, sans espoir de foin . . .

These memories of vagabondage on Flemish roads and through Flemish cities, the very essence of life with Rimbaud, are oddly shot through with recollections of Mathilde. Three poems evoke her, all with English titles: "Green," "Child Wife," and "Birds in the Night": the first is very fine, and is classed with reason amongst the best Verlaine ever produced: "Here are fruits, flowers, leaves and branches, and then here is my heart which beats for you only. Don't tear it with your two white hands, and let the humble gift find favour in your beautiful eyes. . . . On your young breast let my head lie, still echoing from your last kisses, and let me sleep a while since now you repose."

> Voici des fruits, des fleurs, des feuilles et des branches
> Et puis voici mon coeur qui ne bat que pour vous.
> Ne le déchirez pas avec vos deux mains blanches
> Et qu'à vos yeux si beaux l'humble présent soit doux . . .
>
> Sur votre jeune sein laissez rouler ma tête
> Toute sonore encor de vos derniers baisers;
> Laissez-la s'apaiser de la bonne tempête,
> Et que je dorme un peu puisque vous reposez.

Unfortunately, the others fall short of this high level. "Child Wife" and "Birds in the Night" are disastrous. They give Verlaine's story of the rupture with his wife, and he blames her for everything. Was it deliberate hypocrisy or a further illustration of his self-deceptive powers? Probably the latter: he never comprehended his own impulses, and whatever he wanted to be true he thought was so. Mathilde, he declares, lacked patience; she never understood him: "You had no patience. . . . You had no compassion. That's easy to understand; you are so young, my cold sister, that your heart must be indifferent!"

> Vous n'avez pas eu toute patience . . .
> Vous n'avez pas eu toute la douceur.
> Cela, par malheur d'ailleurs se comprend;
> Vous êtes si jeune, ô ma froide soeur,
> Que votre coeur doit être indifférent!

Even now, when he is ready to forgive her (we may well ask, for what?) she refuses to take advantage of the opportunity: "I'm filled with chaste forgiveness"—an odd expression, coming from Verlaine—"not, certainly, joyful, but very calm, even though

I deplore the fact that during these terrible months I've been, thanks to you, the least happy of men."

> Aussi, me voici plein de pardons chastes,
> Non, certes! joyeux, mais très calme en somme
> Bien que je déplore en ces mois néfastes
> D'être, grâce à vous, le moins heureux homme.

"Child Wife," if possible, is even worse: "You'll never have known the light and honor of a strong, brave love, happy in misfortune, calm in happiness and young until death!"

> Et vous n'aurez pas su la lumière et l'honneur
> D'un amour brave et fort,
> Joyeux dans le malheur, grave dans le bonheur,
> Jeune jusqu'à la mort!

Both poems are good examples of just how far his childish disregard for truth could go, a disregard so absolute that it borders on the psychopathic. A child's lies are normal; it cannot distinguish fact from fancy; but Verlaine was a man of twenty-nine. During the rest of his life he continued to sound the same note, until Mathilde, in one of his last volumes, became a "female demon, triple plague, stupid slut, cowardly executioner, a horrible, horrible, horrible woman!"[24]

V *Gunplay and Prison*

The desertion of Rimbaud had been a caprice, a weak tantrum; once settled in Brussels Verlaine could not forget his friend. He tried to be firm: in the frantic letters he wrote he declared that they should never meet again: he was going back to Mathilde, and if she refused to have him he would "blow out his brains." He even wrote Mathilde, who says that she left the letter unopened in a drawer for five years. Elisa, however, rushed to her son at the first word. As for Rimbaud, he had been thoroughly frightened in London, broke and solitary: on July 4 he even sent an imploring letter, begging Verlaine to return to him. But within less than a day his style became laconic and indifferent. Partly because the desperate notes from Brussels showed that his hold over Paul was as strong as ever, partly for the reason that, as he thought matters over, he decided that the time had come to sever relations decisively. Verlaine's sentimentality had long irritated him, as we see from *Une Saison en Enfer;* he had always foreseen that one day he must set forth on his own. Since a break had occurred, and through Verlaine's initiative, it was best to make it permanent.

When Verlaine, unable to bear the separation any longer, summoned him to Brussels by telegram on July 8, he came. But, as he made clear at once, it was only to get money for a ticket to Paris. He refused to change his resolution, and after a day and a night of furious argument, Verlaine bought a revolver and shot him twice. Only one bullet reached its mark, inflicting a slight wound in the wrist. Elisa, now terrified, produced 20 francs for the Paris fare; and the trio set out for the station that very afternoon: Rimbaud sullen, Verlaine pleading, the mother trotting in the rear. The *crime passionnel* is a very real phenomenon, whatever cynics may pretend. There are moments in life when murder is the only remedy for sheer despair. The creative force of love turns destructive in frustration; destruction is the only way of achieving a perverted sort of fulfillment, and Verlaine had reached this stage. "The malice, the cruel flame in his eyes of a fallen archangel!" he recalled many years later. "My fury at losing him was such that I would have liked to see him annihilated."[25] He had sacrificed everything for Rimbaud, and now Rimbaud was walking obstinately toward the station whence a train would shortly carry him away forever. Verlaine thrust his hand into his pocket to seize the revolver. Rimbaud saw the gesture and it was too much even for him. He had been fired at twice already: perhaps the third time the bullet would not miss. He rushed up to a constable nearby and poured out his story. Verlaine was arrested at once for assault with a deadly weapon and locked up for the night.

During the next few days all three actors in the drama made depositions before a magistrate,[26] and shortly thereafter Verlaine was tried on the charge of "inflicting wounds leading to an incapacity for work," an offense provided for in the Belgian legal code. He was found guilty on August 8, 1873, and condemned to two years' penal servitude, the maximum penalty. It was a severe sentence, motivated less by the actual shooting (Rimbaud even withdrew his charges on July 19, anxious to disculpate his friend as far as possible) than by the suspicious circumstances of the case. The two poets had been searched, and their impassioned letters had come to light. The result was a highly suggestive dossier, and matters were not improved when Verlaine, with verbose stupidity, admitted that his wife had just obtained a legal separation charging homosexual relations with Rimbaud. When he tried to appeal the sentence, the Belgian authorities wrote Paris for details of Mathilde's allegations. The answer sealed the poet's fate: his appeal was denied, and from August 27, 1873, until January 16, 1875, he was in jail—first at the Petits Carmes in Brussels, later in the penitentiary at Mons. Elisa and Lepelletier made efforts to have the sentence reduced, but to no avail. He received 175 days off for good behavior and that was all.

As far as poetry went, these months of incarceration were extraordinarily fruitful. The verse produced falls into several categories. First, prolonged echoes of *Romances sans paroles:* "Dame souris trotte," "Je ne sais pourquoi," "Un grand sommeil noir," and "Le ciel est, par-dessus le toit," in which he carried the suggestive, musical side of his talent to its extreme limit. "Art poétique," composed a little later, during the spring of 1874, sets forth his ideas on this type of poetry: like most theories they came after the event, and better define what he had already written than what he was yet to write; the poem was less a beginning than an end—a farewell to the kind of verse for which he had shown such genius. Already, as his weeks in a cell lengthened into months, he was trying out other themes and experimenting in another manner.

As might be expected, memories of Rimbaud obsessed him. He was by turns resentful and fascinated when he recalled the sulky adolescent who had dominated him, heart and mind, and ruined his life. The subject inspired five long *récits diaboliques,* as he called them ("Crimen Amoris," "La Grâce," "L'Impénitence finale," "Don Juan pipé," "Amoureuse du Diable"), a total of nearly 700 lines. They are not among his best work. Inevitably they had to be written: no poet could go through so shattering an experience without trying to make verse of it. But he ought to have handled it in the proper way, the lyric, suggestive way, as he had already treated it in "Ce soir je m'étais penché" and as he returned to it in "Ces passions" and "Laeti et errabundi" of

Parallèlement. Instead, he fell back on the hackneyed Romantic technique of the verse anecdote—even of the Romantic *drame*. The *récits* sound very much like rhymed versions of *East Lynne*. A tender and loving woman (with whom Verlaine identifies himself—a point of some interest) is mistreated by a scoundrelly lover. The male figures are clearly versions of Rimbaud, but so travestied by plot and setting that they are nothing but figments of Verlaine's sentimental inversion.

"Crimen Amoris" is a little more convincing and has been much praised. Form and content are unusual: Verlaine chose lines of eleven syllables instead of the alexandrines of the other *récits*, and he did his best to sketch an impartial portrait of Rimbaud, including both his charm and his intransigence. But the same defects prevail: the piece is so stuck out with meretricious fripperies that genuine feeling is obscured. Adolescent satans are holding an orgy in a Persian palace. Rimbaud, their chief, wears fringes, necklaces, and a jeweled tiara; his demonic speech sums up his ideas as Verlaine remembered them: "I shall be he who will create God. Oh you, Sinners, and you, Saints, sad workers that you are: you knew that there is no difference between what you call Good and Evil. . . . I will break this too-abnormal Bond. We must have no more of that abominable schism! Nor any further distinction between Hell and Heaven! We need love! Death to God! Death to the Devil! . . . Through me, Hell shall sacrifice itself to universal Love . . ."

> Je serai celui-là qui créera Dieu.
> O les Pécheurs, ô les Saints ouvriers tristes . . .
>
> Vous le saviez, qu'il n'est point de différence
> Entre ce que vous dénommez Bien et Mal . . .
> Je veux briser ce Pacte trop anormal.
>
> Il ne faut plus de ce schisme abominable!
> Il ne faut plus d'enfer et de paradis!
> Il faut l'Amour! meure Dieu! meure le Diable! . . .
>
> Par Moi, l'Enfer . . .
> Se sacrifie à l'Amour universal . . .

The *récits* are chiefly interesting because of the religious tendencies they reveal. All turn on problems of sin and redemption: the sins of adulterous women, the pride of satanic men. After Rimbaud has burned the palace and disappeared in its ruins, his theories turn out to have been "vain, vanished dreams," and peace returns to earth, "the peace of the merciful God who preserves us from evil." Verlaine's repentance and conversion began some time before he was aware of it himself.

IV *The Religious Crisis*

We deal here with a theme which accounts for much of his stature as a poet. Religion, as represented by the doctrines of the Roman Catholic Church, had always been part of his life. His parents were not devout, but they attended to his religious instruction and saw that he took his First Communion, which, in later years, he declared to have been "satisfactory": I have already quoted the passage. During his college years, in close association with friends like Lepelletier, he dropped away from the faith and adhered to the agnosticism then in vogue. Parnassianism, when not actively anti-Christian (as in its passion for Greek mythology), was indifferent to matters of belief. But when Lepelletier calls the Verlaine of those years "a rational and intelligent atheist, a complete unbeliever"[27] he gives one more proof that while he admired his friend he did not always understand him. Throughout the poet's life as boy and man there were periodic returns to the Church. Whenever he visited his Grandjean relatives he was in close association with priests who were almost members of the family. One of them, the Abbé Delogne, has described a long and intimate conversation when Verlaine was nineteen: the Father noticed no loss of faith, and since that was a detail in which, as a priest, he was most interested, we may conclude that there had been none: "We talked together for a long time," he wrote Verlaine's aunt, Louise Grandjean. "His nature remains fundamentally good, I'm sure of that, all the more so since he admitted certain weaknesses and confided to me his terror of Paris. The great city is a dangerous place for anybody so lacking in will-power."[28] Still later, Verlaine went through a species of emotional crisis (probably when, as he says, he "felt an urgent desire to change his life" by marriage), and his reaction to it was hardly that of an agnostic: he entered a church for confession and absolution.[29] Faith in God, bound up as it was with memories of his mother and the paradise of infancy, was a part of his nature he could never completely deny. "What is there surprising in the fact that a man should return to the faith of his childhood, to the religion of his ancestors, of his fatherland, to the God his mother taught him and in whose arms his father died?" he wrote Jules Claretie on January 8, 1881.[30] And so, when his blasphemous adventure with Rimbaud wrecked his existence, he turned back to the old consolation.

On April 24, 1874, Mathilde's separation was declared official by a Paris court, giving her custody of Georges. Verlaine had still cherished hopes of getting his wife back, and the news overwhelmed him. Since October of the previous year he had been in solitary confinement (as required by his sentence), and the experience was very painful. "This is above all a prayer, an urgent prayer: *write me* from time to time," he says in a letter to Lepelletier of October 22, 1873: "will you agree to do so every fifteen or twenty days? That's not too much, I hope. . . . My present occupation is sorting coffeebeans; it kills time a little. I am taken out one hour a day, and then I'm allowed to smoke. . . . The courage that upheld me those last days in Brussels is beginning to wear thin. . . . They're very kind to me here and I'm quite as well off as I can be. But my poor head is so empty, so filled as it were with all the chagrins and unhappiness of the immediate past, that I've not yet been able to acquire that kind of somnolence which is, I think, a prisoner's final consolation. That's why I need people to remember me *on the other side of the wall,* and to tell me that they do."[31] In a state like this, Mathilde's rejection was a final blow: he sent for the prison chaplain. After several months' probation, he was once more admitted to communion.

This change had certainly been on the way ever since his incarceration if not before. There were the *récits diaboliques,* with their undeniably metaphysical flavor; and in a letter to Lepelletier of November 24-28, 1873, he mentions writing some *Cantiques à Marie* and some "prayers in the style of the primitive church," one of which bore as title the famous Greek formula: "Jesus Christ, Son of God, the Saviour": "All-powerful, just and holy, you saved Jonah, you saved Tobias. Save then our hearts besieged by evil, save us, O Lord, and confound the impious":

> Tout puissant, tout fort, tout juste et tout saint
> Tu sauvas Jonas, tu sauvas Tobie.
> Sauve notre coeur que le mal enceint,
> Sauve-nous, Seigneur, et confonds l'Impie![32]

As the first of his religious efforts the poem does not lack merit; there is genuine emotion in the lines. And now that he had received absolution from the prison Chaplain, the new source of inspiration reached peak force: "Mon Dieu m'a dit," the dialogue with Christ in ten sonnets which later became the central element of *Sagesse.* He sent the poems to Lepelletier on September 8, 1874: "I assure you that I *feel* every word of it. A man has to go through all I've seen and suffered these past three years, humiliation, disgust—and everything else!—to feel how admirably consoling, reasonable and logical this religion is—and how terrible and how tender. Ah, yes—terrible! But man is so evil, so truly *fallen* and punished by his very birth!—I say nothing of the historic, scientific and other *proofs* which are positively DAZZLING."[33]

These sonnets are usually considered the summit of his work, although they are not his most popular compositions. Most readers, asked to quote a typically "Verlainian" poem, would probably choose something from *Fêtes galantes* or *Romances sans paroles.* In collections like those he was not only exquisite but strikingly original. Religious poetry is in an austere category of its own, beset with limitations. The poet who ventures on it deals with ideas which are beyond dispute; and if he is too original, he ceases to be orthodox. Verse like "Clair de Lune" has no end in view but our pleasure; it does not try to "prove" anything. Piety, on the other hand, can easily turn didactic, irritating the reader with devout complacency or doctrinal onslaught. Verlaine's success under these conditions was extraordinary, and he achieved it through a combination of technique and temperament, in equal measure. The "Mon Dieu m'a dit" sonnets return to the method first evident in "Mon Rêve familier." There is the same deliberate awkwardness, the same repetition of verbs *(aimer),* the same low tone and *rejet* from one line to the next, producing a similar effect of spellbound adoration: "God said to me: My son, you must love me. You see my pierced side, my heart that shines and bleeds, and my wounded feet that Magdalene bathes with tears, and my suffering arms beneath the weight of your sins, and my hands!"

Mon Dieu m'a dit: Mon fils, il faut m'aimer. Tu vois
Mon flanc percé, mon coeur qui rayonne et qui saigne,
Et mes pieds offensés que Madeleine baigne
De larmes, et mes bras douloureux sous le poids
De tes péchés, et mes mains!

The effect is a combination of intense ecstacy and mystic surrender. Terms of light abound—light rising into a crescendo of brilliancy:

. . . Mon coeur qui rayonne . . .
. . . l'amour monte comme la flamme . . .
. . . mon amour monte sans biaiser . . .
. . . ô Vous, toute lumière . . .
. . . l'assomption dans ma lumière . . .
. . . ô ce lit de lumière . . .
. . . le feu qui dévore . . .

And the very simplicity of the style, it's almost conversational tone, produces a more powerful effect than any amount of pompous phraseology: "Lord, it's too much! Truly I dare not. Love whom? Oh! No! I tremble and dare not. Oh! Love you, I dare not, I will not! I'm unworthy. You, the great Rose of the pure winds of love, oh You, the hearts of the Saints, You, who were the Jealous God of Israel, You, the chaste bee who lights on the unique flower of half-opened innocence,—What, *I, I,* be able to love *You?* Are you mad, Father, Son and Holy Ghost? . . ."—"You must love me. I am Those Madmen you named, I am the new Adam who devours the old man, your Rome, your Paris, your Sparta and your Sodom, just like a famished beggar throwing himself onto horrible foods . . ."

—Seigneur, c'est trop! Vraiment je n'ose. Aimer qui? Vous?
Oh! non! Je tremble et n'ose. Oh! Vous aimer, je n'ose,
Je ne veux pas! Je suis indigne. Vous, la Rose
Immense des purs vents de l'Amour, ô Vous, tous,

Les coeurs des Saints, ô Vous qui fûtes le Jaloux
D'Israël, Vous, la chaste abeille qui se pose
Sur la seule fleur d'une innocence mi-close,
Quoi, *moi, moi,* pouvoir *Vous* aimer. Etes-vous vous,

Père, Fils, Esprit? . . .

—Il faut m'aimer. Je suis Ces Fous que tu nommais,
Je suis l'Adam nouveau qui mange le vieil homme,
Ta Rome, ton Paris, ta Sparte et ta Sodome,
Comme un pauvre rué parmi d'horribles mets . . .

Nor are these the only merits of the "Mon Dieu m'a dit" cycle. A more sophisticated poet, learned in the niceties of the creed, would have been hard put to resist the temptation of stuffing them into his lines. Verlaine's very childishness, his inability to understand anything but his own feelings, were positive advantages. He speaks entirely as a human being with no hint of dialectical smugness. In this way only Villon can be compared with him, the Villon of the "Epitaphe." All his remembered past—regrets for lost happiness and frustrated love, desire for protection, surrender to a stronger will—are fused with the tenets of the Athanasian Creed into an experience both personal and universal. Few poets have expressed so much, and even fewer in terms of such enduring beauty.

CHAPTER 3

The Struggle for Faith: Sagesse

I *New Projects*

FOR eight years following his release from prison, Verlaine made a sincere effort to change his life. He had thought about Mathilde a good deal during his months in a cell, and as soon as he was liberated, he wrote her asking for a reconciliation. She answered with a flat refusal: she would not so much as see him. As for the literary world, his position was not much better. A few friends remained faithful: Lepelletier, Blémont, Delahaye (he had come to Paris to see Rimbaud in 1872, met Verlaine, and they remained in touch thenceforth); but the younger generation which was to welcome him so warmly a decade later was still in its teens. Men of his own generation, scandalized by his prison sentence, were resolutely icy. In September, 1875, when a new number of *Le Parnasse contemporain* was to appear, Verlaine sent in some poems afterwards published in *Sagesse*. Two of the judges, Coppée and Banville, abstained from voting; the third, Anatole France, refused in scathing terms: "No, the author is ignoble, and his verses are the worst we've seen."[1] Paris, furthermore, was a dangerous place for the new convert. He found the easy, ever-present temptations of Bohemian circles hard to resist. In desperation he fled back to the Church: it was a refuge from the lusts of the flesh and the scorn of his contemporaries. He applied for entry to a Trappist monastery at Chimay, Belgium. The idea was grotesque, but fortunately the abbot was a man of sense. He allowed the penitent to stay a fortnight, then told him firmly that he had no vocation.

It was as though circumstances were forcing him into the next step: an application to Rimbaud. Their relations, of course, would be very different than in the past: this was the first point he made. He would convert Rimbaud, save his soul: "Let us love one another in Jesus," he wrote when he proposed a meeting.[2] Rimbaud was in Stuttgart, teaching and learning German; he had already dubbed Verlaine "Loyola" when he heard of his conversion. If he now agreed to see him it was through curiosity, not friendship. He wanted to find out how the new piety would resist a few drinks and the memory of shared pleasures. Verlaine reached Stuttgart in a state of emotional turmoil, after eighteen months' enforced chastity in prison. They met and stepped into a bar. Three hours later, as Rimbaud put it in a letter to Delahaye of March 5, 1875, Verlaine had "denied his God and made the 98 wounds of Our Lord bleed."[3] The drinking ended on a riverbank outside town. The younger man was quite lucid: if they reached this deserted spot he had planned it so. He was waiting for Verlaine to make a sexual advance, and when it came he reacted as he had planned: he knocked him senseless and left him to get back to Paris on his own. They never met again.

Such is the story as it has come down to us; it is perhaps exaggerated. Rimbaud ends his letter by saying that Verlaine remained with him for two and a half days "in a very reasonable state of mind, and I then persuaded him to return to Paris so that he could go to England to complete his studies."[4] Even if this is not the whole truth, it hardly suggests a fist fight. The two poets had gone to London in 1872 with the vague idea of studying English and giving French lessons; Rimbaud spent some time there again in 1874, while Verlaine was in prison, looking for a position in a Scottish or English school. Perhaps Verlaine had a teaching project in mind when he set out for Germany and hoped to persuade Rimbaud to share the idea. The account of their Stuttgart interview has been generally accepted since, and can scarcely be refuted at this late date. But it probably needs toning down.

II *Stickney*

At any rate, by the end of March Verlaine was in London and had contacted a teachers' agency. He did not have to wait long. There was a vacancy for a French and drawing master at a grammar school in Stickney, Lincolnshire, and his application was successful. He remained there for a year, from March, 1875 to March, 1876. It was a calm and relatively happy interlude. He lodged at the house of the school principal, William Andrews. They were soon on good terms, and Verlaine also struck up friendly relations with George Coltman, the local Anglican rector. He had never had much contact with Protestants, and he was therefore surprised to find that Coltman had no anti-Roman prejudices and quite approved his desire to attend mass every Saturday at the Catholic chapel in neighboring Boston. His pupils were well-bred, polite and docile; and local society made him welcome. "The circle of my acquaintances has grown larger," he wrote Delahaye on April 29, 1875. "I'm now teaching our fair tongue to the four daughters of a neighbouring doctor. It's not exactly like El Dorado, but thank heaven I've few needs! To live quietly in some province or, if I may, travel slowly through all this country, plus Scotland and Ireland . . . that's the end I have in view. . . . My life is extremely calm, and I'm very well satisfied that it is so: the one thing I need is calm. I've not *even yet* sufficiently triumphed over my past idiocies . . . especially my idiocies of Brussels, *July 1873*. . . . But at least I've been lucky enough to see matters clearly, and what an intellectual reward! What metaphysical sight I've got now!"[5]

During these quiet months he composed many of the poems of *Sagesse* as they appeared five years later. At the time of his release, he intended to print his prison verse in a single volume, *Cellulairement*. But not finding a publisher, and the poems increasing in number, he eventually distributed them through several volumes, especially *Sagesse, Amour,* and *Jadis et Naguère*. Other plans preoccupied him as well, as his letter to Delahaye shows: "My sacred poem will be immense—dealing with the Virgin. Probable title: *Le Rosaire*. From Adam to Eve to the present day: all civilizations, all legends. . . . I've just about got the plan worked out; it is entirely theological. . . . I shall also find the opportunity to write some things in prose: history, criticism, etc. . . . My patriotic book will be short and simple. I hope to be able to send you some bits of it soon. I dare to believe that it will be new, very gentle, very touching, and, as far as possible, very French and not bawdy, very naive, of course, and I shall do my best to be absurdly sincere." And as the letter also shows, all his good resolutions and high projects could not liberate him from his sensual cravings. The past dominated his memories, particularly as it was symbolized by Rimbaud. Throughout the *Corres-*

pondance, Rimbaud's name crops up again and again. The above letter is typical: despite its devout protestations it concludes with: "If you've any news from Stuttgart or anywhere else, let me know what it is, and if you write there, send a cordial handshake on my part." Nothing could exorcise the old spell, not even when, late in 1875, Rimbaud wrote asking for money and hinting at blackmail if it were refused.[6] Refused it was, and Verlaine set down his shock in a poem afterwards included in *Sagesse,* "Malheureux! tous les dons," to which I shall return in a moment.

Life at Stickney, in brief, for all its surface calm, was profoundly tormented. The triumphant faith of "Mon dieu m'a dit" struggled with all sorts of seductive recollections. Paris continued to draw him like a sexual magnet: on the few occasions he ventured there, he nearly succumbed to temptation. "Paris, October, 1875, on the brink of a relapse," we read on the manuscript of one sonnet, "Les faux beaux jours"; and on another, "La vie humble": "Paris, October 1875, after a severe confession."[7] The last half of 1875 seems to have been especially difficult. When Delahaye visited him at Arras during the summer holidays, he found that he was keeping a photograph of Rimbaud in the family album, facing Mathilde's; and if we compare the dates of the poems and letters he wrote at this period, we find that evocations of Rimbaud and supplications to Christ and the Virgin alternate beneath his pen. It was not hypocrisy; in a subtle way it was not even a battle between opposites. His nature was so highly keyed, so responsive to nervous stimuli, that sexual desire absorbed and dominated him beyond the experience of most men, producing a spiritual and moral tension analogous to religious ecstasy itself. His cravings were both intricate and interdependent.

Physical sensation can produce, in certain circumstances, a sort of carnal euphoria which is an escape from reality, a spiritual evasion akin to mystic experience. Verlaine sought much the same thing in religion as in sexuality—shelter and protection—and had he been able to find some brand of faith which combined the two as twin manifestations of the Deity (Hinduism, for example) he would have been perfectly happy. But the orthodox Christianity he professed told him that sex was wrong, and sex refused to admit the verdict. He was not the first man caught on the horns of this dilemma, but he was certainly one of the worst fitted to cope with it.

Had his faith been sustained by dogma or reasoned conviction, had he been familiar with any of the moral therapy by which priests and saints, as keenly solicited as he, have been able to sublimate their torment, he might have resisted better. But in that case he would not have been Verlaine. "When I suffer, when I enjoy, or when I weep," he said once, "I see nothing in my instincts which obliges me to understand why."[8] The whole man is in the phrase. Emotional habits of this sort hardly match the settled conviction necessary to belief. A saint may also be a sinner, but he never forgets that salvation depends as much on moral stamina as on God; a core of certainty in the depths of his soul remains constant however widely desire and personality may fluctuate around it. This was not Verlaine's case. His whole nature was fluid, obscure, undefined, with no central point of reference and no possibility of attaining one. His days at Stickney grew more and more restless. In March, 1876 he resigned and tried to set up as a free-lance French teacher in Boston, with the aid of Father Sabela, the local Catholic priest. The experiment led to nothing, and after a rather unpleasant year at a Catholic school (St. Aloysius, Bournemouth), he was back in France in September, 1877.

II *Notre-Dame de Rethel and Lucien Létinois*

Another post offered itself almost at once—a mastership in literature, history, geography, and English at the Institution Notre-Dame de Rethel, in the Ardennes region (Rimbaud's province). It was a Catholic college, largely staffed by ecclesiastics. At first all went smoothly: "Excellent food; private room; no prying, usher-like duties; nothing, in fact, which suggests the university set-ups, the secondary schools or municipal colleges. . . . Most of the teachers (Latin, Greek, mathematics) are priests and naturally I'm on the best of terms with these gentlemen. They're cordial, simple and good-humored. . . . I've got peace, calm and liberty to see and act—an enormous benefit, that! The salary is reasonable."[9] He found the semimonastic atmosphere particularly congenial: it provided just the sort of haven he needed from the impulses of his nature. In a burst of optimism, he decided that he was quite rehabilitated: the old Adam was tamed.

During the spring of 1878, hearing that his son Georges was sick, he wrote the Mautés and asked to be allowed to visit. Mme Mauté had always liked him and she received him alone at the bedside; neither Mathilde nor her father appeared. This brief encounter heartened him, and as he finished the poems of *Sagesse* he sent them to his wife: it was a way of courting her. Of course the obstacles in the way of a reconciliation were formidable. The Mautés took his protestations with a grain of salt: after what they had seen of Verlaine, they doubted whether he could ever reform, and in any case while family rows might be forgiven, it was quite another matter to take him back after the public scandal and his trial and sentence. Nevertheless, had he persisted, shown that his repentance was genuine and lasting, his marriage might have been re-established. If these tentative contacts came to nothing, his own conduct was to blame.

Notre-Dame de Rethel was not quite so safe as he ingenuously supposed. The first pitfall was alcohol. He had resisted the English pubs, but in France liquor was an element of the daily scene: wine appeared at meals in the Notre-Dame refectory, and all members of the faculty, clerical as well as lay, kept bottles of cordial in their rooms. In other words, the gateway to perdition was legitimately open. Verlaine's dipsomania was classic: in our time he would have had to choose between Alcoholics Anonymous and skid row. One drink led to another: before long he was slipping into town every afternoon for absinthe and coming back so fuddled that he could not meet his classes. Nor was alcohol the only danger. His students represented another. How, with his sensuous temperament, sharpened by five years' chastity, could such a man long associate with teen-age youths and not be roused? He had not been teaching a month before he singled out a boy of seventeen in his English class—Lucien Létinois, sent to college by his father (a peasant farmer in a neighboring town, Coulommes) in hopes that he might better himself through education. He had the frank, clear-eyed charm of adolescence, and his accent—a country burr—was not unlike Rimbaud's.[10]

Critics and biographers haved discussed this passion at length, and several of them are convinced that it was a guilty one.[11] We have no proof either way. Given the circumstances, however, it is at least possible that technical chastity suffered no damage. Verlaine was devout at this period, and so was Lucien, reared as a simpleminded bumpkin. Religion was one of the bonds between them: the poet assumed a mentor-like, father-like pose (for a while he even talked of legal adoption): he inquired into his young friend's moral state, advised frequent confessions, attendance at mass. It was an easy way of making contact, but once initiated it had to be kept up. Any attempt at overt seduction would have scared the boy off. Verlaine had to "sublimate" his instincts; in subsequent letters, conversations, and poems he was forever waxing lyrical over the paternal nature of his affection and Lucien's spiritual qualities. It was a prolonged attempt at moral disinfection, and to some extent it succeeded.

But the victory fairly reeks of suppressed lechery, all the more distasteful for the bogus piety in which it is cloaked. Suppose Lucien cross-eyed or hump-backed: would Verlaine have admired his soul and thought of him as a son? If corruption never took place it was through fear and not virtue. How often the poet must have been on the brink of an avowal or a compromising gesture—to be choked back at whatever cost in nervous suffering. The relationship was the kind of sentimental disaster that overtakes many homosexuals: a dubious compound of tenderness, frustration, and downright misery. In every way it was a worse experience than the orgy with Rimbaud. There had been no pious ambiguity about that: it was frankly sensual and it gave Verlaine freedom and a chance to write great verse. But his relations with Lucien were false from the start. Nor were they justified by any kind of intellectual exchange. Decent and unpretending though the boy was, he knew nothing of poetry and his ideas were extremely limited. His sole function (for which, of course, he cannot be blamed) was to sink Verlaine into four years of libidinous hypocrisy.

In the spring of 1879 the teacher's drinking became so bad that the school fired him;[12] and at the same moment Lucien failed his examinations and was told that he could not return. (There may also have been gossip about his close association with Verlaine: colleges like Notre-Dame are keenly alive to such complications.) In order to keep the boy under his thumb, Verlaine wrote Andrews at Stickney and persuaded him to engage Lucien as a French master. At the same time he applied to the London agency and received a position at the Solent Collegiate School at Lymington, near the Isle of Wight. Duties began in September,

1879. The Mautés who, after his visits the previous year, had expected to hear more of him, were astounded by his silence. He dropped them with complete indifference: it was as though they no longer existed. The new passion had blotted everything else from his mind.

He adapted easily to the Lymington environment, but Lucien was less happy at Stickney. He was a poor disciplinarian and he could not teach. His incompetence was so obvious that Andrews terminated his contract in December. On receipt of the news Verlaine resigned his own position, told the young man to meet him in London, and rushed to the capital. He was in an agony of apprehension, not because of the teaching failure (an irrelevancy), but because Lucien, in one of his last letters, had confessed that he was involved with a girl. We know practically nothing of the affair. Delahaye says that it was a mere flirtation (one of Lucien's students); Verlaine took a more serious view: "Virtuous and religious as he was, with the entirely *filial* regard he had for me, he told of his sin (a truly grave one) and on my urging and not without resistance—very natural at his age and given the circumstances—broke completely with the woman and went to confession,"[13] though just what he meant by "sin" is a question, since he maintained later that Lucien died a virgin. But sin was not what upset him most. He was mad with jealousy, face to face with the homosexual's eternal enemy, woman, a rival all the more formidable inasmuch as Lucien, given that same "filial" attitude toward his old master, was totally unaware of the pain he was causing. A poem in *Amour* (written five years later[14]) deals with the London meeting, which took place on Christmas Day, 1879: "The hateful obscurity of the gayest day of the year, in the monstrous city where our destiny was decided! . . . Remorse for mortal sin was constricting our lonely hearts. . . . Then our despair was such that we forgot the earth, and, thinking of Jesus alone . . . our faith got the upper hand and illuminated us with a supreme light":

> O l'odieuse obscurité
> Du jour le plus gai de l'année
> Dans la monstrueuse cité
> Où se fit notre destinée! . . .

Un remords de péché mortel
Serrait notre coeur solitaire . . .
Puis notre désespoir fut tel
Que nous oubliâmes la terre . . .

Et que, pensant au seul Jésus . . .

Notre foi prenant le dessus
Nous éclaira du jour suprême . . .

What do the lines mean? They have been interpreted in the worst sense, and of course it is conceivable that, exasperated by months of sexual suspense and further provoked by the thought that his prey had very nearly lavished on some wench the things he himself dared not ask, Verlaine may have taken the ultimate step. But, quite apart from the fact that such a step was by no means sure of success, might even provoke a rupture, the reference to "mortal sin" may be interpreted in a different and more odious light. It was Verlaine's way of defining what was essentially a very innocent flirtation. He used the English girl to scare his disciple, turning a normal incident into a threat of hellfire and damnation. Unabashed sensuality appears almost honorable by comparison.

IV *Farming and* Sagesse

Master and pupil returned to France in January, 1880. Since Lucien could not teach, Verlaine had decided that they would farm together. The boy had grown up on a farm; his father was a farmer. Elisa Verlaine produced the cash, and in March a property at Juniville, near Coulommes, was purchased for 30,000 francs. The poet had achieved one more artificial paradise: he settled down like another Corydon, watching Alexis tend his flocks:

Formosum pastor Corydon ardebat Alexin,
Delicias domini; nec quid speraret habebat.

Or had he really given up hope? With a man like Verlaine we cannot be sure. For a while, however, this sylvan retreat was a success: it gave him leisure and tranquillity; he was able to complete *Sagesse* and had it printed at his own expense in December, 1880.

It is a strange volume. Verlaine chose a massive design—perhaps with the *Divina Commedia* in mind[15]—distributing the poems into three divisions which, with some good will, we can see as approximations to the *Inferno,* the *Purgatorio,* and the *Paradiso.* He intended to tell the story of his struggle for faith, to construct a splendid piece of architecture for which he already had the central pediment: the ten sonnets of "Mon Dieu m'a dit." Unfortunately he was not the man for anything so ambitious. He built a façade around the volcano of his nature, but the central fire is forever glaring forth in a manner which by no stretch of the imagination can be called pious.

We can understand these inconsistencies better if we look into the dating, which reveals how the whole composition was assembled. Of the twenty-four poems in part one, thirteen were written in 1875-76. Part two contains thirteen, and twelve date from 1874 to 1876. In part three, the discrepancy between composition and publication is even wider: fifteen out of the twenty-one pieces were written before 1876 (a few of the sixteen stanzas of "Du fond du grabat" as early as 1871, "Le son du cor" in 1872, and "Tournez, tournez, bons chevaux de bois" had already appeared in *Romances sans paroles).* In brief, of the book's fifty-eight poems, thirty-nine are of 1876 or earlier; and fifteen of them occur in the third part, the general conclusion. Chronologically, *Sagesse* stands on its head, and hence its failure as a chant of triumphant faith.

The moment of conversion at Mons (spring and summer, 1874) had produced the great revelation, "Mon Dieu m'a dit." After that, Verlaine struggled with waning inspiration, further weakened by pressing lusts he found it impossible to control. All the poems and sonnets of part one, written at Stickney or during the summer holidays with his mother at Arras, are disturbed by terror of backsliding; and in self-defense, in a desperate effort to save his faith, he fell back on some rather hackneyed techniques: allegory, an abuse of capital letters: "le Malheur," "l'Amour," "la Chair," etc. His style thickened. The genuine piety of the great sonnet sequence began turning intolerant and dogmatic.[16]

Memories of Mathilde and Georges preoccupied him: in four poems (part one, V, XV, XVI, XVIII) he returned to the theme of his loneliness and asked for pardon, without, however, admitting that the failure of his marriage was in any way his fault. Number V dates from Stickney (1875); the others were composed at Rethel three years later; "We can only offend God, and he alone can pardon. But we sadden our brother man, we afflict, wound him, excite his hatred or make his weakness shed tears, and it's a frightful crime. Oh, sister mine who've punished me, pardon me!"

> On n'offense que Dieu qui seul pardonne. Mais
> On contriste son frère, on l'afflige, on le blesse,
> On fait gronder sa haine ou pleurer sa faiblesse,
> Et c'est un crime affreux . . .
> O ma soeur, qui m'avez puni, pardonnez-moi!

Poem XVIII commemorates the brief visits to Georges' bedside at the Mauté house in 1878; XVI is a return to the musical style of *La Bonne Chanson* and *Romances sans paroles:* "Hear the sweet song which only weeps to please you; it is discreet and light: a shiver of water on moss!"

> Ecoutez la chanson bien douce
> Qui ne pleure que pour vous plaire.
> Elle est discrète, elle est légère:
> Un frisson d'eau sur de la mousse!

His comment on the piece when he sent it to Charles de Sivry shows how completely he had abandoned this earlier manner: "It seems to me entirely stupid, and quite without talent, I fear," —a judgment which M. Antoine Adam defines as "a scandalous commentary. . . . We're warned, alas! Whenever, at Rethel, Verlaine finds once again the pure inspiration of the past, he is the first to make fun of it."[17] However this may be, and whatever the value of the poems to Mathilde throughout *Sagesse*, we can only appreciate them when we forget the circumstances of their composition. Verlaine may have believed himself sincere at the time he wrote; perhaps he really wanted his wife back. But when *Sagesse* was published, he was living at Juniville with Létinois. What would he have done had Mathilde taken his lyric complaints seriously and offered to return to him? It was fortunate for them both that such an idea never entered her mind.

As for the second part: "Mon Dieu m'a dit" is one of the finest things of its kind in literature. By a miracle of genius Verlaine combined the personal, anxious style that was peculiarly his with the symbolism and the doctrine of Catholic Christianity to achieve a nearly unique work. But by 1880 the revelation was six years in the past; and to judge from the three pieces with which he thought fit to preface the supreme moment ("O mon Dieu, vous m'avez blessé d'amour," "Je ne veux plus aimer que ma mère Marie," and "Vous êtes calme") the high tide of inspiration began ebbing fairly early. They were written in 1875-78, and in all three religious expression tends to grow threadbare and conventional.

Plan and order break down most completely, however, in the concluding section. The opening is triumphant, a statement of salvation attained: "Henceforth the Sage can watch the world's scenes; he will pass unmoved through the ferocity of its cities":

> Le Sage peut, dorénavant,
> Assister aux scènes du monde . . .
> Il ira, calme, et passera
> Dans la férocité des villes.

But in the very next poem, "Du fond du grabat," Rimbaud's ghost suddenly rises, and not for the first time. In part one, "Qu'en dis-tu, voyageur?" and "Malheureux! tous les dons," this uneasy spectre had already appeared, demanding and irresistible. Both pieces were written in September-October, 1875, when (as we have seen) Verlaine was increasingly obsessed by memories of his lost friend. The Stuttgart quarrel, even the subsequent threats of blackmail, had not laid the old seduction: "Qu'en dis-tu, voyageur?" addresses Rimbaud directly: he is the "traveler" in question: "What have you to tell me of lands and railway stations? Have you at least gathered boredom there? You, smoking sulky cigars and casting your absurd black shadow on the wall?"

> Qu'en dis-tu, voyageur, des pays et des gares?
> Du moins as-tu cueilli l'ennui, puisqu'il est mûr,
> Toi que voilà fumant de maussades cigares,
> Noir, projetant une ombre absurde sur le mur?

Movement and language owe something to Baudelaire's "Le Voyage"; but whereas Baudelaire is epic, general, universal, Verlaine is purely subjective. There are even hints of jealousy: "Tell me the sort of stories I've already guessed: disillusions. . . . disgusts . . . women!"—the gnawing, questioning jealousy of those who have been left behind. And though throughout both "Qu 'en dis-tu" and "Malheureux" he invoked the Deity and rang in his Christian principles ("If I've been punished, it was just. . . . But I have the firm hope of one day knowing the peace and pardon granted to every true Christian"—"God of the humble, save this child of wrath!")—though he did his best to affect pious disapproval and a high moral tone, the basic theme is in each case the same: as in the days of the rue Nicolet or the months of wandering in Belgium and England, Rimbaud meant liberty, movement, and the intoxication of the unknown: things Verlaine still hankered for. "My eyes were dazzled by the roads," he summed the matter up.[18] He could not suppress the old longing: "Have you no splendid vice,—joyous, shameless—one or several? If yes, so much the better! Set off quickly to battle, and fight boldly, indiscriminately, and put on that indolent visor of yours, which conceals a hatred both unslaked and glutted. . . ." And in "Malheureux!": "The curse of never being weary follows your steps through the world as the horizon draws you on":

> N'as-tu pas, en fouillant les recoins de ton âme
> Un beau vice à tirer comme un sabre au soleil . . .
> Un ou plusieurs? Si oui, tant mieux! Et pars bien vite
> En guerre, et bats d'estoc et de taille, sans choix
> Surtout, et mets ce masque indolent où s'abrite
> La haine inassouvie et repue à la fois . . .
> . . . .
> La malédiction de n'être jamais las
> Suit tes pas sur le monde où l'horizon t'attire.

"Du fond du grabat" takes up this theme and evokes the chaotic pleasures of their mutual vagabondage: "The wind from the hill, the Meuse, the glass drunk along the roads at every inn, the tang of flowing sap, the pipes smoked":

> Le vent du coteau,
> La Meuse, la goutte
> Qu'on boit sur la route
> A chaque écriteau,

Les sèves qu'on hume,
Les pipes qu'on fume!

And the tenth number is even more explicit: sexual memories return with the force of an hallucination: "The sadness, the languour of the human body soften me, melt me, move me to pity. Ah! especially when nightmares strike it, when the sheets mark the skin and twist the hand!"

La tristesse, la langueur du corps humain
M'attendrissent, me fléchissent, m'apitoient.
Ah! surtout quand des sommeils noirs le foudroient,
Quand les draps zèbrent la peau, foulent la main!

Composed like "Qu'en dis-tu?" and "Malheureux!" during the autumn of 1875, these poems almost constitute a Rimbaud cycle; and as though to make his intentions even plainer, Verlaine intended to follow "La tristesse" with the sonnet "Ce soir, je m'étais penché sur ton sommeil" of 1872, as we see from the original table of *Sagesse.*[19] Perhaps at the last moment even he perceived the inconsistency of such an idea, and he substituted the relatively anodine "La bise se rue à travers" instead.

But this small concession is not of much importance. When the scattered poems are grouped together, they show that *Sagesse,* outpouring to Christ though it is, carries in its heart a hymn to Arthur Rimbaud. In 1888, while Verlaine was undergoing one of his periodic bouts of convalescence in hospital, stories of Rimbaud's death reached Paris. (They were premature: he lived another three years.) Verlaine was overwhelmed. "What grieves me most," he told Adolphe Retté who was visiting him in the wards, "is not material cares, but my dreams. Since Rimbaud died I see him every night. I can't accept his death. . . . His art and his face still glow in the depths of my soul. . . . He had a diabolical power of seduction. Memories of the days we squandered wandering the roads, intoxicating ourselves with all the frenzies of poetry, come back to me like a tide heavy with terrible and delicious perfumes. . . . For me, Rimbaud is still a living reality, a sun which blazes in my heart, refusing to be extinguished. . . . That's why I dream of him every night."[20] Some of the phrases ring like echoes of *Sagesse,* almost as though

Verlaine were giving a prose commentary on the volume; Rimbaud had been a living reality long before 1888. Even when he is not directly evoked, he is present by implication.

The rest of the third part is equally eccentric. No less than nine out of twenty-one poems (II-IX, XI) predate Verlaine's conversion of 1874; if they were to be included in *Sagesse* at all, it should have been in the *inferno* of the first section. Unless, indeed, Verlaine intended the references to his trials and tribulations as a kind of summing-up, in the same way as Beethoven touches on each previous theme before launching into the choral ending of his Ninth Symphony. An unlikely theory, but supposing him to have had some such intention in mind, then he was unequal to the design. His approximation of *An die Freude* consists of one poem only, the twenty-first and last of part three: "C'est la fête du blé," a description of the harvest as he saw it during a visit to Fampoux in 1877. It uses the symbolism of bread and wine and thus closes *Sagesse* on a religious chord. Beautiful as it is, however, with lovely effects of light, heat, and color, it is too slight to balance the dark themes and sensuous imagery of what had gone before.

So much for the book as poetic architecture. A writer must be judged not only on what he does but on what he tries to do, and in trying to do too much Verlaine got beyond his depth. But design, plan, and architecture are of secondary importance by comparison with what he nonetheless achieved. The epic tone may flag, the mystic note sour. In their place we have some of the most consummate lyric verse ever written. This is particularly true of such preconversion poems of part three as "L'espoir luit," "Gaspard Hauser," "Un grand sommeil noir," "Le ciel est pardessus le toit," "Je ne sais pourquoi." Here the musical, suggestive Verlaine is in full power, and world literature can show few names to rival his. "Poor pale soul, at least drink this water from the icy well. And then sleep. You see, I am staying by you, and I shall fondle your siesta dreams, and you shall sing like a cradled child."—"The sky is above the roof, so blue, so calm! A tree above the roof rocks its branches":

> Pauvre âme pâle, au moins cette eau du puits glacé,
> Bois-la. Puis dors après. Allons, tu vois, je reste,

Et je dorlotterai les rêves de ta sieste,
Et tu chantonneras comme un enfant bercé.
. . . .

Le ciel est, par-dessus le toit
Si bleu, si calme!
Un arbre, par-dessus le toit
Berce sa palme . . .

In *Sagesse* he gave final expression to the verbal genius he had shown since first he began to write. He was to compose fine verse still, but the vein that was so peculiarly his was nearly exhausted. *Sagesse* is the watershed of his work: a summit on one side, on the other a decline. His first books led up to it; his last, with their weaknesses of style and content, are foreshadowed in its defects; and through no accident the best poems are those that were written first.

Dogmatism, as I have suggested, is the most serious flaw. It breaks out like a rash in more than one poem—eleven and twelve of part one, for example, where the free-thinkers and anticlericals of the period are stigmatized as "poor little fellows who know how to prove by A plus B that two and two make four." Veraline's religious convictions had been tending this way for some time. At the moment of conversion he was interested in God alone and his relationship with God. But like all the emotionally retarded he had a craving for absolutes. Tranquil belief was not enough: he wanted a strident piety, an excuse for devout exhibitionism. And just at this moment the political situation in France supplied an excuse for it.

The Third Republic was in full reaction against the Catholicism of the fallen empire, and anticlerical agitation flourished. Verlaine thought himself fit to join this combat on the side of the angels. As he completed *Sagesse* he was also working on *Voyage en France par un Français,* the "patriotic book" he had mentioned to Delahaye five years before, in 1875. It has no value as propaganda and even less as literature. But besides showing how far Verlaine could go in pursuit of a fixed idea, it throws an interesting light on certain aspects of French thought: in its way it is almost a caricature of the extreme right. An American Catholic, I suppose, rarely thinks of his faith as tied to this or that political system. But in France, State and Church, "Throne and Altar," have been fused together ever since the Capetian dynasty, with the aid of the clergy, unified the country during the Middle Ages. Even nowadays religious faith often implies allegiance to the dethroned house of Bourbon. Verlaine's political and religious ideas in his youth were alike radical: as a Republican or a Communard, he was automatically a rationalist and an agnostic. Conversion, however, threw him back onto the cog-wheels of tradition, and before long the ancient mechanism drew him in. The *Voyage en France* is an attack on anticlericalism in the name of Rome, and a vituperation of Republican government in favor of divine-right monarchy. He set about rewriting French history in a mood of vehement paradox.

When the Revolution executed Louis XVI, he tells us, it also beheaded the state, replacing the sovereign with a "hydra," "a servile conventicle, violent and monstrous, composed of dizzy and completely empty pates," the National Assembly. The Revolution was the work of Satan; ever since 1789 France has been governed by the Seven Deadly Sins; universal suffrage is "the last word in intellectual degradation," leading to national decadence: "Today, alas! France appears finished, completely finished! The lessons of the defeats of 1870-71 have gone unheeded. . . . Impiety, allied to the republican idea, is making terrifying progress. . . . There is no more reverence, no more family, no more patriotism. Nothing but a craving for shameless pleasures, for complete and utter debauch."[21] Such allegations are hardly worth refuting. And their very bombast owes much to the circumstances of Verlaine's career. At the time he wrote, he was lusting for Létinois and suffering all the torments of enforced chastity. Nothing makes a man more intolerant of other people's vices.

But perhaps the worst section of all is chapter 7, where the great novelists of the period (Flaubert, Goncourt, Zola) are castigated for the "baneful obscenity and deplorable religious ignorance" of their books. The reproach about religion may or may not be true; but as for obscenity, even supposing it justified, did Verlaine have the right to make it in view of what he had already written and was later to write? "I have not spoken of the horrible sensuality with which the works of these gentlemen abound and overflow," he concludes, "nor of the colossal ennui which is inseparable from this most melancholy of sins. It is the double punishment of a literature of this kind and of the readers who encourage it. But what fine and great talents are here dishonoured and ruined—talents we ought to abhor as if they were the plague itself!"[22] Such incoherent strictures are hardly worth discussion. They refute themselves.

V *Downfall*

The Juniville paradise was of brief duration. Debts accumulated and a bad harvest in the autumn of 1881 completed the disaster. Elisa came up from Paris and helped her son manage the liquidation. The property sold for 15,000 francs, a 50 per cent loss. Once again Verlaine's escapism had led him to a dead end.

Back in the capital with the Létinois family, he had to find some other means of holding Lucien. He applied for reinstatement in the civil service, an idea which had occurred to him as early as March 27, 1874, while he was in jail at Mons: "I don't altogether despair of getting back to the Hôtel de Ville. After all, I'm not a deserter, nor a Communard . . . and as for my prison sentence, I dare flatter myself that there's nothing dishonourable about it: it's above all a misfortune, and a misfortune that can be got over.[23] He had once written that he was "fundamentally a child," but even a child has no right to be so ineptly ingenuous. The appointment depended on Charles Floquet, Prefect of the Seine: he was a friend of Lepelletier's, and well-disposed. But he wrote Brussels for a report of the 1873 trial, and the answer was so shocking that all discussion ceased forthwith. Meanwhile, Lucien Létinois had obtained work at an industrial plant in the suburbs at Ivry. There was a typhoid epidemic at the time and he died suddenly on April 3, 1883.

This was one of those blows that shatters even a strong character, and Verlaine was anything but strong. His despair was complicated by a number of emotional factors: had Rimbaud yielded to his solicitations at Stuttgart and then died, the event could have been rationalized as a vengeance of God. But why Lucien? As far as lay in his power, he had loved the boy innocently. When he said he looked on him as a son he was lying, but it was a sincere lie; he believed it himself. And now his very love was a source of remorse: had he left Lucien in peace, never made a friend of him, never pushed him into the English venture or taken him to Juniville and then Paris, he would still have been alive: "That adoption of you as my child . . . was not according to heaven's plan. . . . Now that I think it over, I see that I had no right to choose you as a consolation on my hard road. . . . I should have left you, humble and joyous as you were, in your nest. . . . That adoption was the forbidden fruit; I ought to have passed by in the perfume and the cool of the tree and of the fruit without stopping. Heaven has punished me. I ought! I ought!"

Perhaps he also realized, however obscurely, that the young man was growing tired of the life thus forced upon him. Lucien even confessed as much to Delahaye: "I'm very grateful to Verlaine, and I like him very much because of his goodness to me and his great affection—despite his faults, his irresponsibility and his eternal emotions. . . . But it is certain that it would have been better for us if we had never met him."[24] Sentiments like these are hard to conceal, and the poet must sometimes have noticed moods of sullenness and impatience which all his blandishments could not dispel. Nor could he fail to understand that it would be impossible to keep a normal young peasant forever cloistered in an atmosphere of ambiguous chastity. Verlaine hovered over him like a zealous eunuch guarding a harem beauty: when Lucien did his military service at Châlons in 1882, his mentor took a room in the city and was on hand every day. As soon as the soldier came off duty the same benevolent, officious presence greeted him at the gates of the camp. He could not accept invitations from regimental comrades to a friendly drink or a night on the town, nor take a walk by himself, nor pick up a girl; he had neither comrades nor girl; he scarcely had his own soul. There was only Verlaine, always and everywhere, solicitous and devoted.

The situation was untenable from every point of view; it had to end some way, and short of death the only way was a rupture. Lucien was not twenty-five when he died, and the day when he would become involved with women was not far off. The English girl had been a sure sign. Verlaine had got rid of her, but he would not always be so successful: the future was heavy with threats of jealousy and recrimination. In this sense, Lucien's death spared him much suffering. The idea even comforted him a little as he followed the coffin to the cemetery: "As I followed your white funeral, I said to myself: It is true, God took you back when you were still a joy to him, in the splendor of your white innocence: later on Woman would doubtless have got your ardent heart into her power."[25] For the moment, however, he was plunged in despair, and there was nothing for it but alcohol and debauch. Since Lucien's parents had decided to remain at Ivry, Verlaine got his mother to buy their farm at Malval near Coulommes, and he moved there with her in July, 1883.

The next two years were a deliberate roll in the mire. Lucien's disappearance was less a reason than an excuse, a pretext for dropping all effort and satisfying long-suppressed instincts. With vindictive and self-tormenting relish, Verlaine surrendered to all the anarchic forces of his soul, "my plan of life being traced out line by line by the logic of a malignant Power." He passed whole days in a besotted haze, hanging over the counters of bars and taverns, on the lookout for any ne'er-do-well who would sell dubious favors for a few francs or a glass of brandy. Sometimes the expense was considerable: one of these passing fancies got 1,500 francs out of him to buy a merry-go-round, presumably as a means of earning a living at country fairs: "Tournez, tournez, bons chevaux de bois! . . ." Within a short time the poet was notorious throughout the Coulommes district, and the more he drank the worse his temper grew. He could not wreak his childish sadism on the toughs he picked up. They were only too ready to pay him back in kind: two of them rolled him one night and left him with empty pockets in a ditch. But Elisa was at hand, the eternal martyr; and in March, 1885, neighbors called the police to protect her from her son. The scene was identical with that described by Victoire Bertrand sixteen years before; he drew a knife and threatened to kill his mother. A court at Vouziers sentenced him to a year in prison. Not since Villon, perhaps (and the circumstances are not quite the same) has a major writer wallowed in such degradation. The spectacle of that sinister figure limping with his cane along the dusty roads, asking fellow tramps for a night's shelter or handouts of food and alcohol, is all the more extraordinary when we remember that just at this moment his name was becoming famous.

CHAPTER 4

Finale (1883-1896)

I *Verlaine and the Literary World*

HE might have profited sooner by this changed situation had Lucien's death not shattered his will. When he came to Paris after the Juniville disaster in 1882, he found that, despite his personal eclipses during the previous decade, his work had been steadily increasing in popularity. The literary scene was very different from what it had been at the time of his release from prison. A new generation had reached maturity, to whom the scandals of his life were mere legends, rather glamorous than otherwise. Parnassianism had had its day; there was a growing demand for something more subtle, more musical, and more intimate – the very qualities of *Poèmes saturniens, Fêtes galantes, Romances sans paroles,* and *Sagesse.* The most vocal groups were the Symbolists and the Decadents – young poets ready for a leader and quite willing to offer Verlaine the role. They visited him, opened their reviews to him: *Paris-Moderne, La Nouvelle Rive Gauche, Le Chat Noir, Lutèce.* In July, 1882 he published two poems in *Paris-Moderne,* "Le Squelette" and "Et nous voilà très doux," subtitled as "poems from *Jadis et Naguère,*" his next volume. On November 10 the same review printed "Art poétique," composed in jail eight years before, and this, together with a sonnet "Langueur" *(Le Chat Noir,* May 26, 1883), at once made him a leader of contemporary poetry.

Symbolists and Decadents were seeking a definition of their theories, and they found it in these poems. "Art poétique" especially caused a great stir. Its insistence on the vague, the undefined, the half-perceived, both in style and content, rapidly became characteristic of Symbolist writing: "Music before all else, and to that end prefer unequal syllabification, vaguer and more soluble in the air, with nothing about it of heaviness and pose. . . . For we want the Shade, not the Color, nothing but the shade! Only the shade can unite dream to dream and flute to horn! . . . Who can tell the sins of Rhyme? What deaf child or mad Negro made this cheap jewel for us which sounds hollow and false beneath the file?"

> De la musique avant toute chose,
> Et pour cela préfère l'Impair
> Plus vague et plus soluble dans l'air,
> Sans rien en lui qui pèse ou qui pose . . .
>
> Car nous voulons la Nuance encor,
> Pas la Couleur, rien que la nuance!
> Oh! la nuance seule fiance
> Le rêve au rêve et la flûte au cor! . . .
>
> O qui dira les torts de la Rime?
> Quel enfant sourd ou quel nègre fou
> Nous a forgé ce bijou d'un sou
> Qui sonne creux et faux sous la lime?

All this, of course, is rather a definition of what Verlaine had already done, from *Poèmes saturniens* to *Sagesse,* than of what he was yet to do. He was putting his ideas into practice, summing up, as it were, the first half of his career. The lines have nine syllables, and the rhymes are sometimes on the brink of mere assonance: *chose* and *pose, impair* and *l'air, rime* and *lime.* But Verlaine was not entirely serious; we shall see what he thought of his disciples' imitations of this side of his work.

The same might be said of "Langueur." It too hit the taste of the period and enjoyed a wide vogue. For many years, ever since the triumph of Romanticism, in fact, conservative critics had accused French writers of decadence and compared them with the authors of the declining Roman Empire. The gambit was based on faulty historical and literary analogies: comparisons between Augustus and Louis XIV or Napoleon; a tendency to see the Prussians of 1870 in the light of conquering Barbarians, and nineteenth-century French authors as analogous to Lucan, Petronius, Claudian, and so on. The writers were naturally irritated at first, but as time passed, they began to utilize these strictures as a means to *épater le bourgeois.* Why not be decadent? It was quite as startling as the long hair and red shirts of 1830. Baudelaire declared that a decadent style was a legitimate and even necessary expression of an age and later defined decadent Latin as "the last sigh of a robust person already transformed and prepared for spiritual life,"[1] an idea developed at some length by Théophile Gautier in his preface to the *Fleurs du Mal* (1868), and still further enlarged by later writers, notably Huysmans in *A Rebours* (1884) and Remy de Gourmont in *Le Latin mystique* (1892). In each case a comparison was implied between dying Rome and modern France. "Langueur" sums up all these themes: waning vigor, lusty Barbarians, poetry as vehicle for the exhausted, rueful sensibility of a corrupt world: "I am the Empire at the end of the decadence, watching the great white Barbarians pass by, composing indolent acrostiches in a golden style where the sun's languour dances":

> Je suis l'Empire à la fin de la décadence,
> Qui regarde passer les grands Barbares blancs,
> En composant des acrostiches indolents
> D'un style d'or où langueur du soleil danse.

"People threw the epithet 'decadent' at us like an insult," he told Jules Huret, "I picked it up as a war cry."[2] As in "Art poétique" his gravity was not wholly real; there is more than a hint of benevolent irony. But this did not dampen the enthusiasm of literary circles: "Langueur" was widely read and imitated: it even had something to do with the foundation of two new reviews, *Le Décadent* and *La Décadence*, both of 1886, not to mention an amusing travesty written by one of Verlaine's friends, Gabriel Vicaire: *Les Déliquescences, poèmes décadents d'Adoré Floupette,* in 1885.[3]

Thus, even though Verlaine's Parnassian contacts had long been broken, his growing popularity soon procured him a new publisher. Léon Vanier, like Alphonse Lemerre twenty-five years before, had started a house specializing in contemporary verse. In March, 1884 Verlaine gave him the first volume of *Les Poètes maudits*, containing essays on Corbière, Rimbaud, and Mallarmé. The title, he later explained, might be changed to *Les Poètes absolus*, by which he meant that the poets in question were "pure" poets with no moral or didactic preoccupations in their work. *Les Poètes maudits* was thus another expression of the art-for-art's-sake theories he had first set down in his study of Baudelaire seventeen years previously. None of the essays have much critical value, but the pages on Rimbaud were of great literary importance, containing as they did the first published texts of "Voyelles," "Les Chercheuses de Poux," "Le Bateau ivre," etc. Verlaine had learned the poems by heart or kept them in manuscript among his papers. Without him they might have been lost.[4]

II Jadis et Naguère *(1885)*

The memory of Rimbaud, in fact, dominated these years. It had already broken through the pious façade of *Sagesse;* it now took over Verlaine's inspiration completely: the last half of his new volume, *Naguère,* about a third of the whole, is made up of the *récits diaboliques* written eleven years earlier in prison. Rimbaud is present in other sections of the book also – "Vers pour être calomnié" (the old "Ce soir je m'étais penché sur ton sommeil" of the Belgian and English trip). *Jadis et Naguère* contains much of interest. Nine pieces grouped under the general title of *A la manière de plusieurs* ("La Princesse Bérénice," "Langueur," "Pantoum négligé," and "Le Poète et la Muse") are particularly good. "Pantoum négligé" is a piece of pure, rhythmic nonsense: when he so wished, Verlaine could be as disconcertingly simple as Gammer Gurton, and in poems like this he more than anticipated Gertrude Stein: "Three little pasties, my shirt's on fire. Monsieur le Curé doesn't like bones. My cousin is blond, she's called Ursule, why don't we emigrate to Palaiseaux!"

> Trois petits pâtés, ma chemise brûle.
> Monsieur le Curé n'aime pas les os.
> Ma cousine est blonde, elle a nom Ursule,
> Que n'émigrons-nous vers les Palaiseaux!

"La Princesse Bérénice" is one of those things Parnassians like Heredia tried to do, but Verlaine did it better: "Her tiny head in her delicate hand, she is listening to the song of the far-off cascades, and in the languourous complaint of the fountains she hears, as it were, a blessed echo of Titus' name. She has closed her divine clematis-tinted eyes, the better to see, amidst heroic battles, her tender hero — the most loving of captains; and, Jewess though she is, she feels herself in the power of Aphrodite":

> Sa tête fine dans sa main toute petite,
> Elle écoute le chant des cascades lointaines,
> Et, dans la plainte langoureuse des fontaines,
> Perçoit comme un écho béni du nom de Tite.
>
> Elle a fermé ses yeux divins de clématite
> Pour bien leur peindre, au coeur des batailles hautaines,
> Son doux héros, le mieux aimant des capitaines,
> Et, Juive, elle se sent au pouvoir d'Aphrodite.

Other sonnets are equally fine: "Sonnet Boiteux," "Le Clown," "Le Pitre," "Circonspection," not to mention "Langueur" and "Art poétique." Yet for all its qualities, the volume gives something of a grab-bag impression. It is obviously a collection of bits and pieces: Verlaine needed to publish something, he had the poems on hand, so in they went: verse of a socialist tendency ("Le Soldat laboureur," "Les Loups," originally intended for *Les Vaincus*, a celebration of humble lives), "Les Uns et les Autres," written in 1871 in the rococo style of *Fêtes galantes*. Other poems date from as far back as 1867. The collection is of great importance, supposing he had never printed its contents elsewhere; but the dates of composition show that it belongs to his earlier period. There is no advance into new fields; inspiration was slowing down.

Despite these hints of waning power, however, the book did much for his reputation: by 1884 he was one of the most discussed poets in France. Composers were setting his verse to music,[5] and J. K. Huysmans singled him out for special praise in *A Rebours* the same year. The novel was a brilliant one, it sold well and has been reprinted as a minor French classic ever since. Its praise was thus of much greater importance than anything a critical article might have provided — it had permanency.[6]

II *Slums and Hospitals*

The two years' squalor at Coulommes stands out curiously against all this success: it is hard to say which adds most piquancy to the other. And henceforth this was to be the atmosphere of Verlaine's life. When he got back to Paris in June, 1885, he wrote Elisa, who had taken refuge with her relatives at Fampoux. She had been awaiting news of her son and joined him at once. Both were now penniless. The proceeds of Juniville and Malval had been squandered; nothing remained of Captain Verlaine's little fortune but Elisa's slim pension as an officer's widow and 20,000 francs worth of bonds, which she prudently sewed into her mattress.

The mattress occupied a bed in a house of ill-fame. Verlaine had moved his mother into the Hôtel du Midi, which stands in the Cour Saint-François, a dead-end constructed in part beneath the elevated railroad running to the Bastille. The poet's room was on the ground floor, Elisa lodged above him at the head of a narrow staircase (so narrow that when she died her coffin had to be lowered out of a window). The other tenants were pimps and whores, social outcasts, drug addicts. Some of the details are nightmarish: the floor of Verlaine's room was unpaved and in damp weather it turned to mud. Elisa did not survive the first winter. She died of pneumonia on January 21, 1886. "She had renounced everything," Delahaye sums up her life. "She would follow her boy anywhere, whatever he did – however unhappy, however insane he might become. And if he wanted to die, it would at least not be because she had abandoned him. And the excellent woman kept her vow until she died herself – near her spoiled child, near her master, just like a faithful dog."[7]

Verlaine could not get out of bed to be with her during her last hours. He was paralyzed by hydarthrosis of the knee, a symptom of tertiary syphilis, marked by stiffening and swelling of the joint. Complicated by alcoholism it was to torment him for the rest of his life, and six months after Elisa's death it grew so acute that he had to make his first sojourn in hospital. At that time hospitals were for derelicts and the very poor: to be ill in one or die in one was tantamount to admitting destitution, and for awhile Verlaine's bourgeois instincts resisted. But when his leg began ulcerating and seeping he had to take the advice of Dr. Louis Jullien, who had been treating him at the Hôtel du Midi. He entered the Hôpital Tenon on July 22, 1886. From then on he often returned: when the weeks and months of hospitalization are totaled, it is found that he spent half the last ten years of his life in charity wards – Tenon, Broussais, Saint-Antoine, Bichat, and others.[8]

The wholesome food, warmth and attention soon reconciled him to the life, and he was now such a celebrity that physicians and interns were flattered to tend him. Dr. Chauffart, head physician at Broussais, had read his books and admired them warmly; and his friends found him out and crowded around his bed. He was soon granted special privileges: a night light and freedom to receive visitors in the garden. There was a certain *chic* about the situation. Nowadays it would be called good publicity. Verlaine was one of the finest poets, and he was also a charity patient: the circumstances were picturesque, and he accepted them with glee. He was once again free from responsibility, as during his childhood: the ward became another facet of his legend, like the Brussels drama and his sexual irregularities. He savored this paradox of squalor and glory and exploited it with characteristic exhibitionism. His fame had passed the boundaries of France: he received invitations to lecture abroad from admirers in Belgium, Holland, and England. These expeditions were profitable: in 1892-93 he made over $500 lecturing, no mean sum at the time. The texts of some of his speeches have reached us and they are not worth much; but the very fact that he was invited to give them enhanced his glory: he was becoming something more than a French poet – a universal one. During his days in hospital he lay propped on pillows writing his lectures, working on book reviews, short stories, and articles, composing verse.

The poetry – Verlaine could never be consistent – was alternately mystic and salacious: elegies to the Virgin Mary or lecherous odes to his trollops and his homosexual companions.

For he was still as sexually inflammable as ever, and though he continued religious, he no longer attempted to be chaste. Within weeks of Elisa's death he had taken up with one of the prostitutes at the Hôtel du Midi, Marie Gambier. She was followed by a host of others of whom the best known, because his relations with them lasted longest, were Eugénie Krantz and Philomène Boudin ("Esther"). They were typical whores, sentimental, mercenary, unbalanced, and foul-mouthed; each had a long history of the sidewalk and the *maison close* behind her and was well past her prime. They provided Verlaine with the rather gamy delights he had always craved, generously spiced with the masochism that was an indispensable ingredient of his sex life. He could only love passionately when he was somewhat misused, when the idol proved enigmatic and withdrawn, not to say positively malignant. Mathilde had bored him with devotion, but this was hardly the case with Philomène and Eugénie. They squabbled over him, cheated him, and periodically decamped with other men – pimps or clients. He knew what was going on, knew that Philomène took his money to buy young lovers, that Eugénie was a vulgar termagant. It made no difference: he loved them both with senile violence, even to the point of offering Philomène marriage. He used to send whichever was living with him at the moment to Vanier's office with a few lines of verse and scrawled request for cash: September 24, 1890: "Mlle Krantz, in whom you can confide utterly, whom I adore, who prevents me from doing all sorts of foolish things and takes care of me and my affairs in such a wonderful way, has been kind enough to undertake to call on you for the five francs I need urgently." – October 25, 1892; "Mlle Philomène, in whom, decidedly, I've put all my confidence and all my friendship (good sense, kindness and probity, she!) will give you the sonnet due you. Please give her 10 francs."[9] Eugénie happened to be in charge when he died and was able to enjoy an almost official prestige as his recognized concubine. Had he lasted longer, Philomène might have had her place.

III *Prose Works*

His output under these conditions was, paradoxically, enormous. From *Jadis et Naguère* until he died (a period of eleven years) he produced a large quantity of prose and fifteen collections of verse.

The prose is bad. Some of it, like *Mémoires d'un veuf,* written 1882-86, would probably never have seen the light had it not been for Edmond Lepelletier, who had worked himself into an important critical position on the staff of papers like *Le Réveil* and *L'Echo de Paris,* and was able to get Verlaine's contributions accepted. Even the critical articles (there are a fair number: book reviews, sketches, a second volume of *Les Poètes maudits,* 1888, which includes a self-portrait under the anagram "Pauvre Lélian" which has stuck to him ever since) are mediocre by comparison with the 1865 study of Baudelaire. *Mes Hôpitaux, Mes Prisons,* and especially *Les Confessions* contain useful biographical material; they have no other merit. The same is true of the short stories: we read them for the hints Verlaine lets drop about himself. Three or four are worth examining in this light.

Louise Leclercq (1886) is a good example of his inability to write fiction. It is also, curiously enough, an attempt to imitate Zola – to rewrite Zola from a Roman Catholic point of view. The heroine, Louise, was raised by her parents, mercers at Batignolles, in an atmosphere of strictest piety. Her father had never been an anticlerical, "never yielded to the terrible corruption of modern society, a result of the press and public morals . . . of which the most striking trait is a brutal denial of God and a consequent destruction of all spiritual values." She received a superior education, reading only the *Annales de la Propogation de la Foi,* "that inestimable historical and geographical treasure which, later on, will certainly prove to be the most important book in every way of the present century."[10] The pious background is emphasized, apparently, in an effort to purge the tale of Zola's "horrible sensuality," as Verlaine called it in the *Voyage en France,* and to demonstrate how a character might be redeemed from sin and transgression by the strength of religious faith. This sequel is hardly achieved. However pious Louise may be, her beliefs have no effect on her conduct. She is often *bored* (Verlaine's italics) and when she falls in love with a young departmental store clerk, Léon Doucet, she yields to him at once. "Useless to explain how the disaster took place," the author writes prudently, thus sparing himself a lengthy piece of psychological analysis. "Louise fell a victim to the malice of reality and to its intrinsic boredom, that boredom which had oppressed her since childhood. . . . Blood and nerves triumphed over her principles. . . . The flame in her blood increased every day, and frank sensuality seized the innocent creature . . . bestial sensuality, the immortal itch of the flesh, the imperious need of the male." This is pure Zola: his men-crazy women, "dominated by their nerves and their blood," his frenzied Rougon-Macquarts, victims of "disasters produced by the nerves and the blood."[11]

Viewed impartially, *Louise Leclercq* almost reads as though Verlaine had set out to prove that religion is powerless to control naked instinct. Louise elopes with her lover. They go to Brussels —a suspicious circumstance, especially when we learn that Léon Doucet's mother gave him a hundred francs for the trip, just as Elisa Verlaine supplied Paul with money when he fled with Rimbaud. There are other echoes of the 1872 escapade: "Louise left her parents without a word of farewell. . . . It was a destiny which obeyed its own laws: all feeling but love had been abolished in her heart." The couple live in sin for several years. Then she hears that her father is dead, her mother paralyzed. She returns to Batignolles, takes over the shop. Her lover joins her; they marry and live happily ever after. An imitation of Zola? Rather a parody. Supposing the tale to have any moral purpose, it is totally clouded. Despite her religious upbringing, Louise can no more resist the lusts of the flesh than can Nana, and the descriptions of her love scenes with Léon are as spicy as anything Zola ever conceived: "She loved her handsome Léon so much, so much! His tenderness, his good nature, his care of her and his obedience enveloped her . . . She was never tired of looking at him, listening to his voice which was both strong and sweet. . . . She swooned with desire at the sight of those eyes, rather small, but so voluptuously designed . . . of that slender nose, a bit tip-tilted, slender, just long enough with its vibrating nostrils, of that strong mouth whose slightly prominent upper lip was shaded with a small line of black silk—which was a moustache; that mouth rich in so many smiles, so many cunning, voluptuous and mad kisses! Short hair with a slight tendency to curl ran in mad locks on a handsome forehead; chin, cheek and neck were of a fine bright pink, and splendid teeth added to the sensual and irresistibly attractive aspect of that head she had kissed so much, caressed with both hands, cradled on her shoulder and in her arms and on her breasts and in her breasts!"[12] The passage is much too luscious to be objective. As usual, Verlaine has identified himself with the woman. Except that, instead of the clinging, fainting lily of the *récits diaboliques* twelve years before, he sketched in Louise the commanding Amazon whom, with another part of his mind, he would also have liked to be. She dominates her lover from first to last, makes the decisions, conducts every step of the plot. In this way she resembles the *femmes fatales* of Rachilde, Mendès, Jean Lorrain, and other contemporary novelists. As fiction, the piece is worthless; as a revelation of Verlaine's secret desires it has considerable interest. And is it not, in some measure at least, a vicarious revenge on Rimbaud?

Pierre Duchatelet (also of 1886) gives Verlaine's account of his conjugal disasters. The hero, a government employee, joins the army for the defense of Paris in 1871. A few details (guard duty, soldiers' argot, ceaseless bombardment) may be accurate enough: the siege as Verlaine remembered it; all the rest is pure extravaganza. Pierre is ordered to the front: he says farewell to his wife. She is a portrait of Mathilde, and the sketch of their lodgings corresponds fairly accurately to the apartment in the rue du Cardinal-Lemoine. To spare her anxiety, he tells her that he has only been called to headquarters and is in no danger. When he comes back after the battle (during which he plays a heroic role), he finds that she has discovered the truth and deserted him—because he lied to her. In desperation he drinks himself into the grave. Nowhere did Verlaine's fancy more completely distort the truth.

A few of the *Histoires comme ça* (1888-90) are more interesting. *Charles Husson* probably describes one of Verlaine's own homosexual adventures. Accosted by a whore, he chooses her pimp instead: "a man made and built for love: a strong face both virile and child-like, pink and plump . . . no trace of a beard except a light gold-blonde fuzz . . . dark-bright hair, curly and rather short; large greenish-blue eyes, very tender . . . large chin . . . a supple but strong body, ample neck and shoulders . . . strong thighs and thick, muscular legs."[13] Here again, perhaps, there are veiled memories of Rimbaud.

Deux mots d'une fille, the least mediocre of these tales, is set in the same milieu, and tells of the poet's relations with Marie Gambier, one of the streetwalkers who lived at the Hôtel du Midi: he took up with her a few weeks after his mother's death. The underworld fascinated Verlaine for several reasons but chiefly because of the sexual emancipation of its denizens, their freedom from all moral bonds. The theme is still popular and has lately reached something of an apotheosis in the novels of writers like Jean Genet and William Burroughs. "I admit that I love these handsome young men, and I admire those valiant women of Joy against whom Society can allege nothing except that they sell pleasure, and what pleasure!" we read in *Deux Mots d'une fille.* Marie Gambier inspired him with almost lyric flights: "She was a light blonde, an ardent and marvelous blonde. Her face . . . was charming with its too-short upturned nose, drinker's complexion, and eyelashes like a white rabbit's . . ."—"Her loosened chemise gave free play to round shoulders, firm breasts with splendid red nipples, plump thighs of a precious satin and a heady perfume."[14] She spent four months with Verlaine, slipping out to work the sidewalks every evening from seven to eleven. He had seen, he says, many women in many postures; but never so beautiful a body. She finally deserted him to go off with a lover who also pimped for her.

These pictures of fin de siècle slum life are engaging and even have a certain charm. But *Deux mots d'une fille* aside—and its value, when all is said, is not great—the main interest of Verlaine's short stories (as of his critical articles) lies in showing that he could not write prose.

IV Amour

There is a twilight quality about his poetry during these years. It is clearly the work of a man who had outwritten himself, even though he was only fifty-two when he died. Technical dexterity he still had: he could turn a stanza with great felicity and was never at a loss for an epithet. But his nervous system, the sensitive fibers which allowed him to feel intensely, had grown dulled beneath the steady mining of alcohol and disease. The colors faded, the subtle harmonies of *Fêtes galantes* and *Romances sans paroles* grew dim and sometimes flat. If a line had not been right in the old days, he knew it instinctively. During the eighties and nineties this critical insight deserted him.

Amour (March, 1888) was composed and added to over ten years or more. It takes up the struggle for faith which dominated his life in the late seventies: many of the poems belong to the period of *Sagesse* and show defects which (as I mentioned) are already perceptible even in that volume. The style loses its poignancy, becomes tired and repetitious: "Grant, of Lord, and dictate my prayer, you all Wisdom and all Goodness, and forever preoccupied with my last hour, you who have loved me through all eternity":

> O Seigneur, exaucez et dictez ma prière,
> Vous la pleine Sagesse et la toute Bonté,
> Vous sans cesse anxieux de mon heure dernière,
> Et qui m'avez aimé de toute éternité.

This poem, "Prière du Matin," is characteristic of the others:

much too long—twenty-five stanzas—with never for a moment the force and ecstasy he had once been able to crowd into fourteen lines. "Ecrite en 1875" is a curious evocation of his penitentiary life. The year and a half at Mons had not been without its compensations. Like childhood, like the hospital wards, prison gave him peace and freed him from all cares and all efforts. "Once I lived in the best of castles. . . . It was a true and good peace, that hard bed, that single chair and table. . . . Twice a day or three times, an austere servant brought my meals and left silently. . . . It was liberty—the only true kind!—*Liberty without its burdens*—[the italics are mine] It was dignity in safety! A place I regretted almost as soon as I left it."

"Un Conte" is interesting because it contains the only honest confession he ever made of his responsibility in the breakup of his marriage: he admits that he was "a brute, a street drunkard, one of those husbands you meet in the slums." But this lucidity was only momentary. His self-deceptive powers soon returned: five poems to Mathilde follow—"A Madame X" (1873), "Un Veuf parle," "Il parle encore," "Ballade en rêve," "Adieu"—where she is once more blamed for all misunderstandings. We might call these poems unjust if so precise a term had any meaning applied to Verlaine. He describes himself as a man "born to please any truly proud soul," a man of "sincere caresses," always ready for "pardon and sacrifice." By a warped process of reasoning, he claimed for himself the qualities he expected in others. The masochism of his relations with Rimbaud and Eugénie was a payment in advance for benefits he hoped to receive, and like most payments of the kind it went unhonored.

Three poems on Wagner are chiefly remarkable for the second one, "Parsifal," a sonnet. George Moore once said that he knew nothing more perfect,[15] and indeed if the lines lack the power of "Mon Dieu m'a dit" or the suggestive music of *Romances sans paroles*, they possess nearly every other quality. There is a deliberate playing with difficulties, a sort of amused disregard for the limitations of prosody and the sonnet technique itself. We are given an exquisite work of art, like a piece of carved ivory or a Renaissance jewel: Verlaine could still be a master when he found a subject to his taste.

The Lucien Létinois cycle of twenty-five poems (one of them, IV, in honor of Elisa Dujardin, was added to the second edition of *Amour* in 1891), commemorates all aspects of that singular episode: the teaching interlude in England (VI, XXIII), Lucien's beauty, moral qualities, athletic prowess (VII, X, XVII, XXIV), his military service at Châlons (XII), the Christmas interview in London (VIII), the farming adventure (XI, XIII, XIV), the poet's paternal affection (XV, XVI), plans for the future (XIX), the boy's death and funeral (I, IX, XX, XXI, XXII), Verlaine's despair (XXV). All are well-written, and two of them, III, an outburst against women in general, and V, "J'ai la fureur d'aimer," are psychologicially revealing.

But despite these merits the over-all impression is unsatisfactory; in a case of this sort mere style is not enough. Just as in the poems to Mathilde, so here we cannot accept Verlaine's protestations: we know too much about the facts. Had he composed an elegy on love—its seductions, its fevers, the menace of time and death—even had he described honestly the sufferings of a thwarted homosexual passion, we could read him without misgivings. But this was not his intention. He wanted to prove to the world (and to himself) that his feelings for Lucien had really been pure and above reproach; that the boy was indeed a son, a substitute for the real son stolen from him by Mathilde. These poems are disappointing: not through inadequacies of rhythm and diction, but in a deeper and more general way, as though the very heart of the matter were somehow wrong. Perhaps cloying piety is the worst single fault: every mention of Lucien provokes references to God and salvation: "My son is dead. I adore your law, Oh Lord. . . . You gave him to me, I return him to you very pure, all steeped in virtue, love and simplicity"—"I put all my pious cares, all the study of which my soul was capable, into confirming his soul in its effort to pray and love"—"Above all my son is beautiful! God surrounds him with light and love, because he was pious and gentle and worthy of the holy Crown reserved for those warriors who combat in Heaven's cause!"—"His real intelligence, and the truly beautiful purity of his eyes and his gestures and his voice, captivated my heart and dictated my choice of him as my son, since my real son, my very entrails, is kept from me"—"Oh, elect of God, pray for me, you who on earth were my good angel."

Mon fils est mort. J'adore, ô mon Dieu, votre loi . . .
Vous me l'aviez donné, je vous le rends très pur,
Tout pétri de vertu, d'amour et de simplesse . . .

Je mettais tout mon soin pieux, toute l'étude
Dont tout mon être était capable, à confirmer
Cette âme dans l'effort de prier et d'aimer . . .

Mais surtout que mon fils est beau! Dieu l'environne
De lumière et d'amour, parce qu'il fut pieux
Et doux et digne encor de la Sainte Couronne
Réservée aux soldats du combat pour les cieux.
. . . sa réelle
Intelligence, et la pureté vraiment belle
Que disaient et ses yeux et son geste et sa voix,
Captivèrent mon coeur et dictèrent mon choix
De lui pour fils, puisque, mon vrai fils, mes entrailles,
On me le cache en manière de représailles . . .

O l'élu de Dieu, Priez pour moi,
Toi qui sur terre étais mon bon ange . . .[16]

Occasionally this devout make-believe bursts under the pressure of desire, and some very unpleasant details emerge—a peeping-Tom interest in the boy's sex life, for example. Verlaine realized that Lucien could not live forever celibate: sooner or later there would have to be a woman. The necessity was a painful one, but he could stand it better if he had a hand in choosing her. He turned matchmaker, the eternal refuge of erotic frustration: "It often happened that, just like a father for a son of his own flesh, I liked to dream of a charming future for you—a perfect, beautiful and good bride. I sought, I found, I was never really satisfied: so occupied by your needs that I even put myself into your place":

Il m'arrivait souvent, seul avec ma pensée,
—Pour le fils de son nom tel un père de chair,—
D'aimer à te rêver dans un avenir cher
La parfaite, la belle et sage fiancée.

Je cherchais, je trouvais, jamais content assez . . .
Prenant ta cause enfin jusqu'à tenir ta place.

This sort of thing was totally abnormal—not a preoccupation with Lucien's happiness, but a vicarious form of sexual contact. We can well believe that he was "jamais content assez". A wife for Lucien was the last thing he wanted, and had the young man waited until Verlaine arranged his marriage he would have waited in vain.

The relationship between the pair, in brief, was as unsatisfactory as any human relationship can well be, and *Amour* reveals its disastrous effects on them both. Lucien was isolated and enslaved; Verlaine's life became a bad comedy of baffled lust and pious shams. Even more serious, the supreme vindication, the vindication of poetry, was here withheld. For all its fine passages, *Amour* is a mediocre work. Verlaine was trying to deceive himself. Perhaps he succeeded: his capacity for illusion was pretty well unlimited. But he also tried to deceive his readers, and there he did not succeed at all.

V Parallèlement

He may not have been as blind as the book makes him sound. There was a streak of lucidity in him sometimes, as when, even though he laid all the blame for the downfall of his marriage on Mathilde, he could write "It's I who cuckolded my wife and in a mighty funny way, too!"[17] As he completed *Amour* he was working on a very different type of volume, *Parallèlement* (1889), as we see from his letters at this time. They make his intentions clear: January 16, 1886: "I've got some wonderful projects for *Parallèlement*. . . . What a piece I'm adding to it! in a parallel way, of course, to a very different one for *Bonheur* . . ."—November 22, 1886: "I'm working hard on *Amour* and *Parallèlement* . . ."—January 13, 1887, to his editor Vanier: "Enclosed two poems, one for *Amour*, the other for *Parallèlement*."—February 15, 1887: "*Amour* will appear . . . and after that, *Parallèlement*." —May 1, 1887: "*Amour* and *Parallèlement* are finished, and I've sent them to Vanier."—October 26, 1887: "A volume of mine to appear, *Amour*. It's Catholic, not clerical, although very orthodox . . . *Parallèlement* will follow, a completely 'profane' collection—pretty strong stuff—but, I think, amusing."—January 5, 1888: "I'll be publishing in a few months a book entitled *Parallèlement*, of an extreme and as it were ingenuous sensuality, which will be a contrast to the very sincere Catholic mysticism of *Sagesse* and of another volume, *Amour*, which is also going to appear." And in *Les poètes maudits, deuxième série* (1888): "Pauvre Lelian's work separates, after 1880, into two distinct parts, and the prospectus of his future books indicates that he's adopted this system and will continue to publish, if not simultaneously . . . at least in a parallel way, works based on totally different ideas: books where Catholicism displays its logic . . . and others entirely worldly: sensual . . . and filled with the pride of life."—Finally, January 11, 1892, to Raulin, editor of *L'Univers:* "I've completed an entirely personal and, I think, unique work in French poetry: the history, as it were, of a conversion. . . . Four volumes: *Sagesse, Amour, Bonheur* of a naive Catholicism . . . and finally *Parallèlement,* which, as its title indicates, is, by comparison with the earlier professions of faith, a brutal, or, if you wish, odious confession of many sensual faults. This harsh book . . . is not the last by any means. The last of the tetralogy in *Bonheur,* a severe and entirely Christian book."[18]

If not the last volume he wrote, *Parallèlement* is his last collection of genuine poetic value, and an unusual effort (unusual for Verlaine) to face the problems of his dual nature: his parallel interest in religion and sensuality, hetero- and homosexual love. Like all his best work, it is the fruit of a crisis. He had taken to religion with passion and tried to apply its precepts to his relations with Lucien. Then Lucien died; Mme Verlaine died; the flesh took revenge in unbridled lechery. The failure was complete: all his struggles had ended in disaster. He remembered his years of faith and chastity with regret, but he could no longer deny his proclivities. And success had come, bearing unexpected results in lecture tours, admirers around his hospital bed, discerning praise from good critics and ready money from a host of sources. He was now too illustrious to be allowed to die in a gutter. Friends contributed to his upkeep; Maurice Barrès organized a committee to provide him with a pension of 150 francs monthly; the Ministère de l'Instruction Publique sent him 1,500 francs in three instalments during 1894-95; editors like Vanier and Deschamps (of *La Plume*) paid reasonably well for his contributions. He was a spoiled child again, endlessly indulged; and he became slightly callous. Since people esteemed him, let them do so without illusions: let them accept him as he was. There was a good deal of satisfaction in dropping all pretense and forcing the world to take him on his own terms.

Parallèlement, therefore, opens truculently with a reprint of *Les Amies,* the six Lesbian sonnets of 1867. After twenty-two years, censorship was less touchy and they could now be published openly. They are pretty in a languorous, epicene way: "Such, their moist arms entwined about their supple waists—a strange couple pitying other couples—such, on the balcony, the young women stood dreaming. Behind them, in the depths of the alcove rich and dark, vivid as a melodramatic throne and filled with perfumes, the Bed, unmade, opened in the shadows":

> Telles, leurs bras pressant, moites, leurs tailles souples,
> Couple étrange qui prend pitié des autres couples,
> Telles, sur le balcon, rêvaient les jeunes femmes.
>
> Derrière elles, au fond du retrait riche et sombre,
> Emphatique comme un trône de mélodrames
> Et plein d'odeurs, le Lit, défait, s'ouvrait dans l'ombre.

The chief immediate source is probably Baudelaire's "Femmes damnées." But as is always the case in a comparison between the two poets, Verlaine's inferiority is at once apparent. "Femmes damnées" gives a tragic view of a tragic passion, more akin to Racine's *Phèdre* than to *Les Amies.*

The six poems of *Filles,* the second division of *Parallèlement,* are very successful: light-toned evocations of whores, including Marie Gambier, "La Princesse Roukhine": "Who but me could best describe this body, I, its bard and priest, and its humble slave and its master, who would damn myself for it without regret. . . . Fair thighs, erectile breasts, back, loins, belly—a feast for the eyes and the searching hands and for the mouth and all the senses?"

> Et qui pourrait dire ce corps
> Sinon moi, son chantre et son prêtre,
> Et son escalve humble et son maître
> Qui s'en damnerait sans remords . . .
>
> Cuisses belles, seins redressants,
> Le dos, les reins, le ventre, fête

Pour les yeux et les mains en quête
Et pour la bouche et tous les sens?

The deliberate combination of sensuality and religion is, of course, part of the *Parallèlement* theme, and became more and more characteristic of Verlaine at this period.

The bulk of *Révérence parler*, the third section, belongs to the prison years, and was to have figured in *Cellulairement*. The lines are often beautiful, in the earlier manner: "Impression fausse" is typical: "Lady mouse walks, black in the evening's grey, lady mouse walks, grey in the black":

Dame souris trotte,
Noire dans le gris du soir,
Dame souris trotte,
Grise dans le noir.

—The Gammer Gurton note again.

Lunes, the conclusion, contains his last sustained poetry. Parallelism between normal and abnormal love is the theme, and for the first time homosexuality is given the preference. "Explication" celebrates it as morally and emotionally superior to the love of women, and "Autre Explication" takes up the old struggle between Rimbaud and Mathilde on a note of poignant regret for Rimbaud: "What cowards we were to drop each other the way we did!"—"Lâches, nous! de nou être ainsi lâchés!" After distorting the surface piety of even *Sagesse*, Rimbaud now emerged to full view as one of the main inspirations of Verlaine's work, whether prose or verse. Two poems in *Lunes* give the theme in full orchestration: "Ces passions" and "Laeti et erranbundi." And this time there are no devout misgivings nor veiled allusions. The first is a ten-stanza apology for homosexual love, a striking example of Verlaine's ability to handle a scabrous subject with great allusive elegance. The tone is occasionally rather fin de siècle, as when inversion is described as "a pure witness for the soul in the struggle for freedom from oppressive nature." This idea had been popular for some time: sexual perversity had become a characteristic of the dandy and the decadent as they evolved from Romanticism's Fatal Man. The Romantic cult of Nature was replaced by artificiality, implying self-mastery and calculated effect. In this context, abnormality of any sort was a proof of free will: "*Depravity*—that is to say, departure from the normal—is impossible to animals, who are dominated by changeless instinct," Gautier wrote, and later writers echoed him.[19] But in "Ces passions," pederasty is handled so broadly as to be above contemporary fashion and the eccentricities of the lunatic fringe. It becomes legitimate eroticism; and in this way the poem is one of the first things of its kind in modern literature and much more impressive. both in form and content than subsequent work like André Gide's *Corydon.* "These passions which they alone still call loves are indeed true loves, tender and furious, with strange peculiarities which, certainly, humdrum daily loves have not . . . and to fulfill all their desires, each partner in turn performs the supreme action, enjoys perfect ecstasy—now the cup or the lip and now the receptacle—languid as night itself, fervent as day. . . . Their gambols are open and gay. There are no crises: vapors, nerves. No: only courageous games, and then, with tired and happy arms about each other's neck, mutual sleep, less tired than close, interrupted by revivals."

Ces passions qu'eux seuls nomment encore amours
Sont des amours aussi, tendres et furieuses,
Avec des particularités curieuses
Qui n'ont pas les amours certes de tous les jours . . .

Et pour combler leurs voeux, chacun d'eux tour à tour
Fait l'action suprême, a la parfaite extase,
—Tantôt la coupe ou la bouche et tantôt le vase—
Pâmé comme la nuit, fervent comme le jour.

Leurs beaux ébats sont grands et gais. Pas de ces crises:
Vapeurs, nerfs. Non, des jeux courageux, puis d'heureux
Bras las autour du cou, pour de moins langoureux
Qu'étroits sommeils à deux, tout coupés de reprises.

"Laeti et erranbundi," which follows, is like a sequel to "Qu'en dis-tu, voyageur?" and "Du fond du grabat" of *Sagesse.* It gives in nostalgic detail an account of the two years with Rimbaud, all spite and quarrels forgotten. Verlaine composed it about the same time as his hospital conversation with Adolphe Retté, shortly after the false report of Rimbaud's death in 1888. "Our travels were bold (how stodgy the present seems by comparison!)—by steamers and express-trains. . . . We fled lightly through the light ether, two happy phantoms! Passion, insolently satisfied beyond measure, intoxicated our minds and senses—gave us everything we craved: youth, friendship, and our hearts were completely free from the wretched thought of women, and from the last of all prejudices. . . . It was the delight of two men living together, better than a model married couple, each contributing his share of strength and faithful sentiment." Even the irksome poverty of the weeks in London, which caused the final break, now seemed glamorous: "Sometimes money was a terrible problem, but we faced it with joy, courage and potatoes. . . . And now people say that you are dead. . . . I won't believe it: dead, you, god amongst demi-gods? . . . Dead, my great radiant sin, all the past that still boils in my veins and my brain, shines and blazes in my eternally renewed fervor? . . . What, dead, the miraculous poem, the sum of philosophy, and my fatherland and my freedom, dead? Never! You live my life!"

Les courses furent intrépides
(Comme aujourd'hui le repos pèse!)
Par les steamers et les rapides . . .

Nous allions,—vous en souvient-il,
Voyageur où ça disparu?—
Filant légers dans l'air subtil,
Deux spectres joyeux, on eût cru!

Car les passions satisfaites
Insolemment outre mesure
Mettaient dans nos têtes des fêtes
Et dans nos sens, que tout rassure,

Tout, la jeunesse, l'amitié,
Et nos coeurs, ah! que dégagés
Des femmes prises en pitié
Et du dernier des préjugés . . .

Le roman de vivre à deux hommes
Mieux que non pas d'époux modèles,
Chacun au tas versant des sommes
De sentiments forts et fidèles . . .

La misère aussi faisait rage . . .
On ripostait par le courage,
La joie et les pommes de terre . . .
On vous dit mort, vous . . .

Je n'y veux rien croire. Mort, vous,
Toi, dieu parmi les demi-dieux! . . .
Mort, mon grand péché radieux,

Tout ce passé brûlant encore
Dans mes veines et ma cervelle,
Et qui rayonne et qui fulgore
Sur ma ferveur toujours nouvelle!

Quoi, le miraculeux poème
Et la toute-philosophie,
Et ma patrie et ma bohême
Morts? Allons donc! tu vis ma vie!

In the fourteen years since "Qu'en dis-tu, voyageur?" Rimbaud the "Traveller" had attained full stature in Verlaine's eyes, and he remained so to the end.[20]

There was another passion behind *Parallèlement:* Verlaine had become interested in an artist-journalist of twenty-five, Frédéric Cazals. They met at Symbolist gatherings around 1885, and from the beginning the poet was ardently attracted. At first Cazals was rather flattered: he was nobody, and Verlaine enjoyed universal fame: Symbolists and Decadents looked on him as a god. But his desires were turbulent, and he made no effort to hide them. Literary circles were soon rocking with gossip and innuendo. On August 20, 1888 (we know the date from a note written two days later[21]) Verlaine drank too much and made his intentions clear. Cazals had no homosexual tendencies, and he said so frankly, perhaps emphatically. A spate of imploring letters followed from Verlaine: lachrymose cries for pardon and promises of self-restraint. But though the poet beat a retreat he did not give up hope: during the ensuing months he wrote endlessly, expounding the purity of his intentions, talking about God and the Virgin Mary, trying to awaken Cazals' pity: "I'm sick; I see clearly that I've nothing to look forward to—you're the only true and deep affection I have in the world."—"What caused all my lapses? Heredity, education? I was good and chaste. Drink, I think: it developed the parasite of Lubricity in my flesh—originally intended to be normal! . . . I'm feminine, which explains many things!"[22] Verbiage of this kind might deceive a Létinois, but it had no effect on a man who had grown up in the Paris streets and knew all the ropes. Cazals saw clearly what the pious chatter concealed and he remained unmoved. Verlaine had to accept the refusal; passion waned and was replaced by a friendship which eventually became one of the consolations of his last years. But the episode is an interesting revelation of his state of mind as he composed *Parallèlement*.

VI *Last Collections*

The same intense lubricity characterizes nearly everything else he wrote. "The *Parallèlement* vein has got hold of me," he said in a letter to Cazals (October 4, 1889). "Extraordinary, that sensual vein. Even the things for *Bonheur* show it."[23] For while religious themes still preoccupied him, he was interested in them more as "parallels" than as exercises in piety. And in any case piety as a source of inspiration was well-nigh exhausted. *Bonheur* and *Liturgies intimes* (1891, 1892) are often banality at its worst: verse sermons, with here and there attempts to sublimate Cazals into a sort of Christ figure *à la* Létinois, or final outbursts of resentment against Mathilde.

Femmes and *Hombres* (1890-91) are more interesting. If we accept pornography as a legitimate subject for literature (and if we do not we exclude a large amount of work from Shakespeare on down) then we must admit that Verlaine succeeded where better men have failed. It was one of his most extraordinary triumphs, and without it the picture of him would not be complete: besides being the exquisite lyricist of *Romances sans paroles* and the sublime mystic of *Sagesse,* he is also the poet who invested obscenity with genuine lyric beauty. I said a moment ago that *Parallèlement* was his last good sustained verse: the statement needs qualifying in the light of *Femmes* and *Hombres.* Anybody can write smut; but smut which also has poetic value is the rarest of achievements.

The rest of his production during these years hardly deserves much attention. His trulls were always good for a poem or two: Eugénie is the Muse of *Chansons pour Elle* (1891), Philomène of *Odes en son honneur, Elégies,* and *Dans les Limbes* (1893-94). *Chair* (1895) was written for them both. None of the verse is good. Neither lady could qualify as an Egeria, and even Verlaine realized the futility of draping her in the exquisite harmonic webs he had spun for Mathilde and Rimbaud—supposing him still able to spin them. Each drab was important to him in contradictory ways; each satisfied his confused sexual cravings, always more cerebral than physical. Thus a trollop like Eugénie was something more than a vehicle of coarse pleasures, even though coarse pleasures were a prime consideration: "After our nights of vigorous love, I leave your arms tempered like steel; your rich caresses are what I need. . . . Your love gives bravery to all my being, just like wine."

> Après nos nuits d'amour robuste
> Je sors de tes bras mieux trempé,
> Ta riche caresse est la juste . . .
> Ton amour répand la vaillance
> Dans tout mon être, comme un vin.[24]

But she was chiefly useful in abolishing all his doubts and fears, drowning him in a sea of pure instinct, even freeing him from his preoccupation with God: "Let's be scandalous with no more care than a stag and his hind in the woods. Let's get rid of all shame. Let's even exaggerate a bit, and, if not cynical, let's at least be scandalous without further hesitation. Above all, no talk of literature! To the devil with readers, authors, publishers . . ."—"I used to be a mystic, and I am no longer. (Woman has retaken possession of me utterly.) . . . Oh, what a blessèd time it was when I was a mystic!"

> Soyons scandaleux sans plus nous gêner.
> Qu'un cerf et sa biche ès bois authentiques.
> La honte, envoyons-la se promener.
> Même exagérons et, sinon cyniques,
>
> Soyons scandaleux sans plus nous gêner.
>
> Surtout ne parlons pas littérature.
> Au diable lecteurs, auteurs, éditeurs . . .
> . . . .

Je fus mystique et je ne le suis plus
(La femme m'aura repris tout entier) . . .
O le temps béni quand j'étais ce mystique![25]

His sentiments for Philomène were perhaps a little more tender, a little less brutally sexual. "I love and always shall love that woman," he admitted.[26] She was grossly stupid, but her character had nothing of the settled malignancy Eugénie showed on occasion. Her vices were less dramatic: she was heedless, shiftless, bovinely resigned to the servitudes of prostitution. Verlaine found her rather touching: "You're not a virgin, alas! But you're still a martyr, not for God, but for anyone you like (what are people laughing at?), because of your bleeding heart which remains sublime. Courageous you are, poor dear adored one, in order to bear so much unlimited pain with that pride which adorns a victim, and with all that pardon both joyous and patient."

Tu n'est pas vierge, hélas! mais encore martyre
Non pour Dieu, mais pour qui te plut (qu'ont-ils à rire?)
A cause de ton coeur saignant resté sublime,
Courageuse, tu l'es, pauvre chère adorée,
Pour supporter tant de douleur démesurée
Avec cette fierté qui pare une victime,
Avec tout ce pardon joyeux et longanime.[27]

If less dreadful than Eugénie, however, she was no more successful as an inspiration to his flagging Muse. The poems he wrote her border on the grotesque: "And now, the Buttocks! Goddesses of goddesses . . . Repose in delight, calm gaiety, mischievous dimples, just like little laughs, and a touch of perversity in what majesty!"

Et maintenant, aux Fesses!
Déesses de déesses . . .
Du repos en liesses,
De la calme gaîté,
De malines fossettes,
Ainsi que des risettes,
Quelque perversité
Dans que de majesté![28]

Given the circumstances, few things could be stranger than this vivacious lubricity. One thinks of aging Philomène, of Verlaine with his stiff knee and his ulcers. The vision is not agreeable. As for the realities of that superannuated love-making, one prefers not to think of them at all.

Verlaine quite realized what a figure of fun he cut; but one of the advantages of being a great poet was that he no longer needed care what people thought or said. "Let them shout as they wish: 'It's ridiculous! Idiotic! A dotard like that! To what lengths the flesh will go!' . . . The world may gossip about me as much as it likes. I love you, dotard that I am; yes, you: even though you're scarcely young any more. I love you with a love like spring, a late love, with a vigor both reflective and deliberate: it blends my decline with your maturity."

> Les gens crieront ce qu'ils voudront: "C'est ridicule,
> Idiot! Un barbon! Où la chair nous accule,
> Pourtant! . . ."
> Va, toi! Le monde en vain de moi caquettera,
> Je t'aime, moi, barbon, toi, plus une ingénue,
> D'une amour, comme de printemps, tard survenue
> Et d'un élan, aussi, médité, concerté,
> Mariant mon déclin à ta maturité.[29]

The verse of all the last collections is often marked by this same jocose desperation, as tired and rueful as the sexual desire that inspired it. Time had worn Verlaine out, turned the ecstasies of youth into salacious mania. Here and there a daring assonance or a sad bit of humor crops up: pale sparks which are insufficient to arrest the reader's attention. The same is true of the volumes of occasional pieces: *Dédicaces, LeLivre posthume, Epigrammes, Invectives* (1890, 1893-94, 1894, 1896). Good poems occur here and there: the sonnet to Rimbaud, and particularly the last of all the poems, "Mort!" in which Verlaine's genius spoke out once more on the very brink of the grave. But the general impression is of talent not merely waning but on the point of exhaustion.

For ten years his health had been deteriorating. "Rheumatism, heart murmurs, the beginnings of diabetes and the last stages of syphilis," he wrote Gabriel Vicaire from the Hôpital Broussais on

November 13, 1891, "a nice programme, isn't it?"[30] Added to this and perhaps even more serious, was the eternal drinking. When he contracted pneumonia in January, 1896, the case was hopeless. He was living with Eugénie at 39, rue Descartes, and he died there on January 8. The house now bears a plaque to commemorate the event. He was so famous that the funeral turned into a triumphal celebration. Expenses were paid by friends and by the Ministère de l'Instruction publique; there was a profusion of flowers, and telegrams arrived from all over the world. Some time later Eugénie petitioned the ministry for a grant to cover her expenses. As everybody knew, she had battened on Verlaine for years: he owed her nothing. Nevertheless, such was his prestige that even his aging harridan excited reverence. She was given 100 francs, "for strictly exceptional reasons." The episode has the same outlandish humor of so much else in Verlaine's career.

CHAPTER 5

The Summing-Up

A short life, less than fifty-two years; yet its output was considerable. From *Poèmes saturniens* until his death, Verlaine averaged one volume of poetry every eighteen months, plus a fair quantity of prose. Only the most prolific giants like Hugo have done better. What is its value?

Like all literary work, it must be judged by a double standard: what it meant to its age and what it means nowadays. Verlaine's contemporaries thought of him as an innovator: he had added new techniques to poetry and helped free it from traditional rules. Critics of the period were forever stressing this point. Their articles almost give the impression that before Verlaine verse was so fettered with regulations that little of any value was written.[1] Yet his much-advertised novelties were hardly extensive—experiments of one kind or another with the prosody of the time. It was strict: whatever political and social changes France went through after the Renaissance, the rules of versification remained constant. The language has no tonic accent, and certain techniques were therefore judged necessary to distinguish poetry from prose: a rigid scheme of alternate masculine and feminine rhymes, and a steady, pulsing beat, obtained by lines in equal numbers of syllables. Four, six eight, and ten were common, but the standard measure was twelve: the famous alexandrine, skewered on a median caesura like a butterfly on a pin. Here are a few examples chosen at random over a period of two hundred and fifty years:

> . . . France, mère des arts, / des armes et des lois . . .
> . . . Rendre le ciel jaloux / de sa vive couleur . . .
> . . . Beauté, mon beau souci, / de qui l'âme incertaine . . .
> . . . Je le ferais encor, / si j'avais à le faire . . .

> ... Je commence à rougir / de mon oisiveté ...
> ... Périssent tes serments / et ton Dieu que j'abhorre! ...
> ... Elle a vécu, Myrto, / la jeune Tarentine ...

From mid-sixteenth century until the dawn of the nineteenth, in short, most French poets used the same prosodic machinery to express themselves.—Surely one of the strangest examples of literary conservatism on record.

The Romantics claimed emancipation. But though they lived at a time when traditional values had been challenged or overthrown, they used their opportunity timidly. Victor Hugo was the most revolutionary of them all: he liked to boast that he had put a red cap of liberty on the dictionary and "dislocated" the alexandrine:

> ... J'ai mis un bonnet rouge au vieux dictionnaire ...
> ... J'ai disloqué ce grand niais d'alexandrin ...[2]

By which he meant that he had enlarged the vocabulary and placed the caesura elsewhere than at the sixth syllable, a proceeding known as *enjambement sur la césure.* This was not much. He was also fond of *rejet*—overflow of sense and rhythm from one line to the next:

> Mais c'est affreux d'avoir à se mettre cela
> Dans le tête ...[3]

Baudelaire too liked stylistic tricks of this kind; examples of both may be found in his work, and they interested Verlaine as we know from the essay he wrote on his predecessor. When he wanted authority to justify his own tinkering with Classical machinery, he found it in Hugo and Baudelaire. In this sense his verse is a further development in the direction of twentieth-century *vers libre.*

He also liked to compose in lines of five, seven, nine, eleven, and thirteen syllables:

> ... Une aube affaiblie ...
> ... C'est l'extase langoureuse ...
> ... Tournez, tournez, bons chevaux de bois ...
> ... Dans un palais, soie et or, dans Ecbatane ...
> ... Il faut, voyez-vous, nous pardonner les choses ...

It was the *impair* he recommended in "Art poétique," "vaguer and more soluble in the air, with nothing in it of heaviness and pose." But how much importance did he really attach to the formula? He later advised his disciples "not to take 'Art poétique' too seriously, it's only a song"[4]; and much of his best verse, with less of heaviness or pose than anything else he wrote (most of the 'Ariettes oubliées' in *Romances sans paroles,* for example) is not always composed in *impair.*[5]

He also liked to rhyme weakly or adequately instead of richly, according to another precept enunciated in "Art poétique": "You'd do well, as you spend your efforts, to make Rhyme behave: if we don't watch it, where will it lead?"

> Vous ferez bien, en train d'énergie,
> De rendre un peu la Rime assagie:
> Si l'on n'y veille, elle ira jusqu'où?

For the benefit of those not familiar with these minutiae, a rhyme between "fidèle" and "nouvelle," where only one syllable echoes the other, is "weak"; "tige"and "vertige" (final vowels supported by identical consonants) are "adequate"; and "destinée" and "matinée," where each word has two sounds of equal value, are "rich." A great deal of noise was made over this point even before Verlaine's time, and I doubt very much whether any poet worthy of the name paid it much attention. Victor Hugo even turned the matter to ridicule with an extreme example of rich rhyme—where *every* syllable echoes the other:

> Gall, amant de la reine, alla, tour magnanime,
> Galamment de l'arène à la tour Magne, à Nîmes.[6]

If poets used only rich rhymes, they would not write much; most of Racine's rhymes are adequate at best and often weak; and the Romantics, in the long run, did as they pleased, using whatever rhymes came to hand—weak, adequate, or rich. So did Verlaine. Weak rhymes were part of his recipe for blurring the contours of meaning and creating a vague and dreamy impression: a specious theory which, again, he did not always practice. The rhymes of some of his most suggestive verse are frequently adequate. And while a few of the experiments he made with half-rhyme and assonance are mildly interesting—

Les variations normales
De l'esprit autant que du coeur
En somme témoignent peu mal
En dépit de tel qui s'épeure . . .

—at his most revolutionary in this respect he was clearly being facetious:

J'opine
Pour les deux en même temps . . . ni ne
Dis mot . . .[7]

On this point as well he did not wish to be taken too seriously, and when his disciples began carrying "Art poétique" to its logical extreme and discarding rhyme completely, he was filled with misgivings: "The poem in question is *carefully* rhymed. . . . Use weak rhymes or assonance if you will, but use one or the other: French verse is impossible otherwise."[8]

More important was his treatment of the caesura. In numerous cases he ignored the sixth-syllable rule:

L'inflexion des voix chères qui se sont tues.
Laisse-la trompeter à son aise, la gueuse!
De la douceur, de la douceur, de la douceur!
Amour qui ruisselais de flammes et de lait . . .
Il faut m'aimer! Je suis l'universel Baiser . . .
Ces passions qu'eux seuls nomment encore amours . . .

Occasionally he even bridged it with a single word:

Et la tigresse épouvantable d'Hyrcanie . . .
D'une joie extraordinaire: votre voix . . .

Most striking of all, however, was the way he used *rejet* from one line to the next. The effect of rapt ecstasy throughout "Mon Rêve familier," "Mon Dieu m'a dit," and later poems like "Parsifal" is one result:

Car elle me comprend, et mon coeur, transparent
Pour elle seule, hélas! cesse d'être un problème
Pour elle seule, et les moiteurs de mon front blême . . .

> Je ris, je pleure, et c'est comme un appel aux armes
> D'un clairon pour des champs de bataille où je vois
> Des anges bleus et blancs portés sur des pavois . . .
>
> Parsifal a vaincu les Filles, leur gentil
> Babil et la luxure amusante—et sa pente
> Vers la Chair de garçon vierge que cela tente
> D'aimer les seins légers et ce gentil babil . . .

It is not too much to say that in this respect he was the most accomplished of French poets. None of the others ever used the technique with such consummate art—certainly not Hugo, not even Baudelaire.

There is little more to say of him as an innovator. He owed his reputation in that respect less to any real changes he introduced than to the fact that he was dealing with so rigid a structure that the least alteration appeared revolutionary. And here too the admiration of his disciples somewhat disconcerted him. "I'm having trouble with my Decadents," he wrote Dr. Jullien in 1888: "I'm very much inclined to drop gently all those brats, who are decidedly compromising."[9] Three years later he expressed his disapproval in even stronger terms: "To have poetry you've got to have rhythm. Nowadays people are writing lines of a thousand feet! It's no longer verse, it's prose and sometimes mere gibberish!"[10] He drew back from the new schools in consternation: refused to write for their manifestoes, refused to admit that he even knew what Symbolism was. "Symbolism? I don't understand. Must be a German word, eh? What the devil can it mean?"[11] A coolness resulted: the young men were offended and began looking elsewhere for a master. "He's too much under Baudelaire's influence," Jean Moréas declared in 1891, adding that he had nothing further to teach contemporary poetry, and that far from being an initiator, he was the end of a line, the last word of a dead tradition.[12]

Verlaine, indeed, was not the sort of man to found a school—even when tempted to it by the flattering imitations of other poets. He had taste enough to see that the imitations were usually mediocre. When Ghil, Kahn, Vièlé-Griffin, Samain, Moréas himself tried to write like Verlaine they labored infelicitously: the attentuated effects of *Fêtes galantes* and *Romances sans paroles* explain much of the epicene posturing and masturbatory languour of Symbolism and Decadence. But he can scarcely be held accountable for these aberrations. He had no desire for disciples and, despite "Art poétique," his talent was too spontaneous to bother with rules and regulations. *"I've formulated no theory,"* he declared in 1890, underlining the words to make his intention clear. "Perhaps that sounds naive, but naiveté seems to me one of a poet's most precious qualities." And again: "Let me dream if I want, weep when I like, sing when the idea comes to me."[13] It was a good definition of his work. Whenever he adopted a program or paid lip service to some esthetic creed or other, he labored in vain. His poetry (as he told Mallarmé) was "an effort to render sensation"[14]; and sensation is wholly personal, all the more so when the writer is a Verlaine, tied to a world of memory and illusion: childhood and his mother's affection, the Metz years, the long holidays with Elisa Dujardin at Lécluze. Throughout his existence, this sinking fund of regret and recollection dominated him; now subconsciously, now openly: each of his sentimental escapades was less an effort to relive the past than to impose it on the present, remaking life according to the data memory supplied. Mathilde, Rimbaud, Létinois, Cazals: each was expected to perform the same role—shielding him from reality, allowing him to inhabit a dream world of his own invention. Which meant carrying out the functions his mother had once assumed. Small wonder that in the long run they all lost patience. Hence the sexual and emotional failure of his life and (paradoxically) hence the success of his art. He was capricious, unstable, uncontrollable, forever on the sensual *qui-vive*, a man impossible in any normal context. But poetry is hardly a normal context, and when he began to write the very qualities that prevented rational adjustment gave his verse its peculiar beauty. He could never transcend himself: his inspiration obeyed nervous impressions, not the summons of conscious will. He had to wait until conditions were right; but when they were, when no preconceived idea or self-conscious theorizing intervened between him and sensation, he commanded one of the most seductive styles in the history of poetry. True enough, his key was minor and his tone low. But these are limitations, not defects, and we could easily make out a case in their favor. Subdued harmonies are often the most alluring of all. They speak to us more urgently and more intimately than other music, and for that reason we listen to them longest.

Notes and References

(All quotations from Verlaine are taken from Verlaine, *Œuvres poétiques complètes* (Bibliothèque de la Pléiade) referred to as Verlaine, Pléiade, or from *Œuvres complètes de Paul Verlaine,* Le Club du Meilleur Livre, 1959, 2 volumes, referred to as *CML.* All Rimbaud quotations come from Arthur Rimbaud, *Œuvres complètes,* Bibliothèque de la Pléiade, referred to as Rimbaud, Pléiade.)

Chapter One

1. *CML,* I, 85.
2. Le Febve de Vivy, *Les Verlaine,* p. 23 *sqq.*
3. "Un simple buveur héréditaire," the phrase used by Dr. Legrain in writing to Joseph Uzanne, Georges' employer. The letter was shown me by M. Yvan Christ. See the appendix to my *Verlaine: A Study in Parallels.*
4. Elisa's daughter-in-law, Mathilde Mauté. Former-Madame Paul Verlaine, *Mémoires de ma vie,* p. 122. Referred to henceforth as "Mathilde." Edmond Lepelletier, *Paul Verlaine, sa vie, son oeuvre* (henceforth referred to as "Lepelletier"), p. 48.
5. *CML,* II, 1152, *Les Confessions.*
6. *Ibid.,* pp. 1095-96, 1130.
7. *Ibid.,* p. 1122.
8. *Les Poétes maudits, deuxième série,* 1888, *CML,* I, 884.
9. *Ibid.,* pp. 1150-51.
10. Letter to Rimbaud of April 2, 1872. See Rimbaud, Plèiade, pp. 281-82. Letters to Cazals of June, 1889 and August 26, 1889, in Georges Zayed's *Lettres inédites de Verlaine à Cazals,* pp. 139, 174.
11. *Les Confessions, CML,* II, 1143, 1155.
12. "The Observer effaces himself completely behind the esthetic effect of his observations." J. H. Bornecque's definition, *Etudes Verlainiennes, Les Poèmes saturniens,* 34.
13. Les Confessions, *CML,* II, 1166-67.
14. Cf. Leconte de Lisle's "Midi," from *Poèmes antiques* (1852):

    Viens! Le soleil te parle en paroles sublimes;

Dans sa flamme implacable absorbe-toi sans fin;
Et retourne à pas lents vers les cités infimes,
Le coeur trempé sept fois dans le néant divin.

15. "Critique des *Poèmes saturniens,*" in *la Revue d'aujourd'hui,* 15 mars 1890, reproduced in Verlaine, Pléiade, pp. 1071-74.

16. Harry Graf Kessler, *Besuch bei Verlaine,* 10 Juli 1895, published in *Insel-Almanach auf das Jahr 1965.*

17. "Charles Baudelaire," *CML,* I, 60.

18. *Ibid.,* pp. 55-57.

19. *Ibid.,* pp. 57-58.

20. Verlaine, Pléiade, p. 1073.

21. J. H. Borneque, *op. cit.,* 87.

22. *Les Confessions, CML,* II, 1097.

23. Denis-Auguste-Marie Raffet (1804-60) was a painter of military subjects.

24. "Perhaps we owe *Fêtes galantes* to the strong impression made on Verlaine by 'La Fête chez Thérèse'. He admired it so much that it was the only poem by a well-known author I heard him recite by heart." Lepelletier, p. 162.

25. *Ibid.,* p. 184.

26. *Ibid.,* p. 83.

27. Stendhal, *Lucien Leuwen,* in *Romans et Nouvelles,* Pléiade, I, 1534. Zola, preface to Dr. Laupts, *Perversion et perversité sexuelles* (Carré, 1896).

28. It is true that Balzac *(La Fille aux yeux d'or)* and Musset *(Gamiani, ou une nuit d'excès*—if the novel is really by him) represent one lady as more aggressive than the other. But nowhere is this side of the matter so emphasized as in "Femmes damnées: Delphine et Hippolyte."

29. See Jean Richer's Freudian interpretation of the poem in *Paul Verlaine,* p. 19.

30. Mathilde got the story from Elisa, who said she had been told by Lepelletier. But who but Verlaine could have been the original source? Mathilde, p. 152; Lepelletier, p. 451.

31. *Mémoires d'un veuf, CML,* I, 701, "A la mémoire de mon ami ***." When first published in *Lutèce,* 1-8 février 1885, this read: "A la mémoire de mon ami Lucien Viotti."

32. To Léon Valade, *CML,* I, 944-45.

33. *Les Confessions, CML,* II, 1169.

34. Lepelletier, p. 83, says that his mother thought Verlaine looked like an ape from the zoo.

35. Mathilde, p. 89.

Chapter Two

1. Rimbaud's famous letter to Paul Demeny, May 15, 1871. Rimbaud, Pléiade, pp. 269-74: "Le Poete se fait *voyant* par un long, immense et raisonné *dérèglement* de *tous les sens.* Toutes les formes d'amour, de souffrance, de folie; il cherche lui-même, il épuise en lui tous les poisons, pour n'en garder que les quintessences . . . Il devient entre tous le grand malade, le grand criminel, le grand maudit,—et le suprême Savant!—Car il arrive à *l'inconnu!* . . . Donc le poëte est vraiment voleur de feu . . . Baudelaire est le premier voyant, roi des poëtes, *un vrai Dieu.* Encore a-t-il vécu dans un milieu trop artiste; et la forme si vantée en lui est mesquine. Les inventions d'inconnu réclament des formes nouvelles." Baudelaire wrote that Edgar Allan Poe had excelled in analyzing the *exceptions* of human life: "Les ardeurs de curiosité de la convalescence, l'hallucination laissant d'abord place au doute, l'absurde s'installant dans l'ntelligence et la gouvernant avec une épouvantable logique . . . le personnage de Poe, l'homme aux facultés suraiguës, l'homme aux nerfs relâchés, l'homme dont la volonté ardente et patiente jette un défi aux difficultés, celui dont le regard est tendu avec la roideur d'une épée sur des objets qui grandissent à mesure qu'il les regarde,—c'est Poe lui-même." *(Edgar Poe, sa vie et ses oeuvres,* 1856, in *Edgar Allan Poe, Œuvres en prose, traduction par Ch. Baudelaire* [Pléiade], 1046-47.) And in a letter of January 21, 1856, Baudelaire defined Joseph de Maistre as "le grand génie de notre temps,—*un voyant!" (Correspondance générale,* Conard, I, 369.) Both passages are worth comparing with some lines in Gautier's Notice to the *Fleurs du Mal* (Calmann-Lévy), page xxx: "Baudelaire . . . sait découvrir par une intuition secrète des rapports invisibles à d'autres et rapprocher ainsi, par des analogies inattendues que seul le *voyant* peut saisir, les objets les plus éloignés et les plus opposés en apparence." The word *voyant* (seer) is italicized in all these texts.
2. He was well acquainted with a certain Auguste Bretagne, an old friend of Verlaine's from Fampoux, living in retirement at Charleville, who added a note of recommendation to the first letter. The point is obscure, since Mathilde subsequently burned all the correspondence. But many years later Verlaine recalled that Rimbaud had written that he was "rather a dirty little guy" *(une petite crasse),* and admits that he found the remark intriguing. "Nouvelles notes sur Rimbaud," *CML,* II, 1289.
3. F. Porché, *Verlaine tel qu'il fut,* p. 122 *sqq.*
4. Rimbaud, *Une Saison en Enfer,* Pléiade, p. 229.
5. Delahaye, *Verlaine,* p. 21.
6. Lepelletier, pp. 261-62.
7. Rimbaud, Pléiade, pp. 756-58. Cabaner is mentioned in a police

report of Thursday, August 22, 1878, as a well-known homosexual: "On me signale parmi les plus fervents adeptes de la 'Rosette' un nommé Cabaner, musicien excentrique . . ." (Now in the Verlaine file at the Préfecture). These police reports are not always reliable: they were sent in by paid spies whose living depended on writing something and who recorded the idlest rumors rather than remain silent.

8. "C'est l'extase langoureuse" and "Le piano que baise" in *La Renaissance artistique et littéraire,* May 18, June 29, 1872.

9. Delahaye, p. 375.

10. Lepelletier, pp. 247-48.

11. Mathilde, p. 195.

12. *Ibid.,* p. 201.

13. Lepelletier, p. 272. The testimony, coming from a favorable witness like Lepelletier, is important.

14. Mathilde, p. 210.

15. *Ibid.,* p. 219.

16. Quoted *CML,* I, 1417.

17. Now in the Verlaine file at the Préfecture.

18. Published in *Jadis et Naguère* (1884) as "Vers pour être calomnié."

19. "Vagabonds" in *Les Illuminations,* Pléiade, p. 190, and *Une Saison en Enfer,* ibid., p. 231.

20. Verlaine's letter to Rimbaud of July 3, 1873: "Cette vie violente et toute de *scènes,*" Rimbaud, Pléiade, p. 290.

21. Lepelletier, IX, *passim,* and *CML,* I, 1014-18. Verlaine seems to have realized how interesting these sketches were: shortly afterwards (in 1872) he included them in a list of his works "now printing" as *Londres: notes pittoresques. CML,* I, 1058.

22. See Verlaine's account of the incident, Rimbaud, Pléiade, 821-22.

23. Verlaine, Pléiade, 1100, and Verlaine's letter of May 19, 1873, in *CML,* I, 1039, in which he explains why he wanted to dedicate the book to Rimbaud. Lepelletier doubtless persuaded him to drop the idea; he had always disliked Rimbaud, and he realized that such a dedication would add fuel to the scandalous rumors then circulating in Paris. The dedication disappeared when the book was printed in March, 1874.

24. In *Bonheur,* 1891.

25. Verlaine's account as he gave it twenty years later to Adolphe Retté. Quoted by J. H. Bornecque in *Verlaine par lui-même,* pp. 86-87.

26. These depositions are reprinted in Rimbaud, Pléiade, pp. 297, 299.

27. Lepelletier, p. 388.

28. Le Febve de Vivy, *op. cit.*, p. 51.
29. His own account as recorded by Delahaye, *Verlaine*, pp. 75-76.
30. *CML*, I, 1151.
31. *Ibid.*, p. 1068.
32. Verlaine, Pléiade, p. 295.
33. *CML*, I, 1090.

Chapter Three

1. Quoted by Enid Starkie, *Rimbaud*, 151-52.
2. Delahaye, pp. 210-11.
3. Rimbaud, Pléiade, p. 307.
4. *Loc. cit.*
5. *CML*, I, 1099 *sqq*.
6. See Verlaine's letter of December 12, 1875 (the last he ever wrote Rimbaud) in *CML*, I, 1121.
7. See the notes to these poems in the Pléiade Verlaine.
8. Jules Huret, *Enquête sur l'évolution littéraire*, 1891. Quoted *CML*, II, 1760.
9. Letter to Lepelletier, November 14, 1877, *CML*, I, 1135. A minor point of some interest in view of Verlaine's career as an English teacher is how much English he knew. I have found no comment by anybody who ever heard him speak it. His reading knowledge was probably good: he went through an astonishing amount of literature, and not all of it easy: Shakespeare, Bunyan, Poe, Swinburne, Goldsmith, Byron, etc. As for his ability to write the language, it left much to be desired. Here are a few examples: to Mrs. Smith, his London landlady: "Madame, I will return to-day in Paris, rue de Lyon, 12. Do you please (as soon as possible) send to me in my box all things which remain in the room again. Your obedient servant, P.V." (Rimbaud, Pléiade, 824).—"Nous cherchons lessons *at people well off's.*" *(CML,* I, 1120).—"Don't you think that it would be possible to me to hope for some money in return for my four 'Paris living?' If such was the case, I could manage in order to write one per week? You could perhaps, if I were not able to-morrow to see you at the 'brasserie,' answer me and deep post a word on the matter. Excuse bad English . . ." *(ibid.,* 1172).—"Je suis malade comme jamais, je ne puis rien garder et not a farthing at home and I want remedies and it is necessary to have five. Eugeny, not withstanding all her courage is out of forces and courage. If it were possible to you, how much thankfull for an immediate money!" *(Ibid.,* II, 1750-51). During his last years he several times asked Mallarmé (also an English teacher) to find him pupils: *CML*, II, 1651.
10. "In every way he resembled Rimbaud a little"—reported by

Cazals, presumably on what Verlaine had told him. Quoted by V. P. Underwood, *Verlaine et l'Angleterre*, p. 326.

11. Porché, p. 299, and Marcel Coulon, *Verlaine poète saturnien*, p. 151, are for guilt; Antoine Adam (*le Vrai Verlaine*, p. 54), for innocence. I side with Adam.

12. This is the account given by F. A. Cazals and Gustave Le Rouge, who should have known the facts: *Les Derniers jours de Paul Verlaine*, pp. 131-32.

13. Delahaye, p. 329; Verlaine, *Amour*, VII, IX; V. P. Underwood, p. 328; and letter to an anonymous correspondent of November 17, 1883, *CML*, I, 1177.

14. The eighth of the Lucien Létinois cycle, published first in *La Revue Critique*, January 27, 1884. Verlaine, Pléiade, 448.

15. Echoes of Dante occur here and there, notably in part three, XII. See Pléiade, 1133.

16. First part, poems XI and XII—attacks on the anticlericals of the period, particularly Gambetta, Ferry, and Paul Bert.

17. *CML*, I, 1142.

18. "J'étais faible . . . les yeux éblouis des chemins," Pléiade, p. 266.

19. *Ibid.*, p. 1133.

20. Retté, as quoted by Bornecque, p. 88.

21. *Voyage en France par un Français*, *CML*, I, 348.

22. *Ibid.*, p. 405.

23. To Lepelletier, *CML*, I, 1078.

24. Delahaye, p. 312-13.

25. *Amour*, IX, Pléiade, p. 449.

Chapter Four

1. Note to "Franciscae meae laudes," *Les Fleurs du Mal*.

2. *CML*, II, 1762.

3. In which Verlaine appears as "Bleucoton," oracle of the Decadents.

4. This was not precisely the first publication of these poems: Verlaine had already given most of them to *Lutèce*, where they appeared in the autumn of 1883. See Rimbaud, Pléiade, p. 870.

5. Bordes and Chausson, 1883-85; later Debussy and Fauré. Porché, p. 273.

6. See Georges Rodenbach's article, "La poésie nouvelle. A propos des décadents et des symbolistes," *La Revue bleue*, 4 avril 1891. And Georges Zayed, p. 21, on the favorable publicity supplied by *A Rebours*.

7. Delahaye, p. 337.

8. See the chronology in Jean Richer's *Paul Verlaine,* pp. 78-79.
9. *Correspondence,* II, letters to Vanier, 166 *sqq.*
10. *CML,* I, 618.
11. *Ibid.,* pp. 625-26. And Zola, preface to *Thérèse Raquin* (1867), preface to *La Fortune des Rougon* (1871).
12. *Ibid.,* pp. 627-30.
13. *Ibid.,* p. 214.
14. *Ibid.,* pp. 237-38, 241.
15. *Confessions of a Young Man* (New York, Modern Library, 1917), 62.
16. Verlaine, Pléiade, 443, 447, 448, 453, 456.
17. Quoted by J. H. Bornecque, "Les Dessous des Mémoires d'un veuf," *Revue des Sciences humaines,* avril-juin, 1952.
18. *CML,* I, 1188, 1210, 1218, 1223, 1227, 1273, 1292, 886; II, 1674; and letter to Dr. Jullien, undated, but probably of this period: "on one side Catholic verses, almost archangelic; on the other licentious passages, more and more sensual, without for that reason becoming sadistic: horrors which make part of a plan, the *tragic program* Baudelaire speaks of." *Correspondance,* III, 376.
19. *Notice* to the *Fleurs du Mal* (Lévy), p. xxvi. I have discussed this question at length in the first chapter of my *Idea of Decadence in French Literature* (Toronto).
20. Here is the list for 1895: Preface to *Arthur Rimbaud, ses poésies complètes; Arthur Rimbaud (The Senate,* London, October); *Nouvelles notes sur Rimbaud (La Plume,* 15-30 novembre); *Arthur Rimbaud, Chronique (Les Beaux Arts,* Ier décembre). Verlaine, it should be remembered, died on January 8, 1896. Throughout all his later years he was capable of evoking the old passion in embarrassing detail. "I remember once, in a pot-house of the rue Monsieur le Prince," Francois Porché writes of these years, "how someone mentioned Rimbaud's name before Verlaine. . . . With a furious gesture he brought his cane down on the zinc and I wouldn't dare repeat the words that came from his mouth. In hiccoughs ending in sobs, in a torrent of curses, there burst forth the avowal of a passion which neither prison, nor time, nor the death of the beloved had been able to extinguish. We watched this madness with the embarrassment of Noah's children watching their father's obscene intoxication." *L'Amour qui n'ose pas dire son nom* (Grasset, 1927), p. 39.
21. Georges Zayed, *op. cit.,* p. 92.
22. *Ibid.,* pp. 111, 118.
23. *CML,* II, 1623.
24. Verlaine, Pléiade, p. 710.
25. *Ibid.,* p. 727.

26. Letter of December 5, 1893, from London, informing Eugénie of his determination to break with Philomène. *CML*, II, 1719.

27. Pléiade, p. 766. Despite this tone of tender pity, there was a strong element of masochism in Verlaine's relations with Philomène—as in all his sexual relations. A few poems further on we read: "You were often cruel . . . but what's that to me, since I believe in you alone and since I'm your thing. You deceive me with Pierre, Louis, etc. I know it; but that's none of my business: I'm only the humble servant of your moods, whether they're gay or sad. If you beat me, slap me, scratch me, you're the master in our house, and I the cuckold, the beaten, and I'm happy and see everything in a rosy light." Pp. 770-71.

28. *Ibid.*, p. 771.

29. *Ibid.*, p .788.

30. *CML*, II, 1670.

Chapter Five

1. "He broke the cruel shackles of versification," "he opened a window," he sought "novelty, and an art that would be a combination of poetry, painting and music . . . a concert in color or a painting in music—a deliberate confusion of genres, a sort of Tenth Muse": opinions expressed by Moréas, Rachilde, etc.; quoted by Martino in *Verlaine,* 188, 193, 201, 189. Mallarmé's opinion was: "The father, the true father of all the young poets, is Verlaine, the magnificent Verlaine, whose attitude, as a man, I find as splendid as his attitude as a writer. Because it is the only possible one at a time when the poet must live outside the law: accept all suffering with so much pride and such a splendid swagger." Conversation with Jules Huret in 1891, reprinted in the Pléiade Mallarmé, p. 870.

2. "Réponse à un acte d'accusation," *Les Contemplations,* 1856.

3. Quoted by Verlaine himself in an essay on Barbey d'Aurevilly, 1865. *CML*, I, 1422.

4. Pléiade, p. 1074.

5. Of the nine pieces in *Ariettes oubliées,* four are in *impair* (I, II, IV, VIII), and in another IX, *pair* and *impair* alternate.

6. Ernest Raynaud, *Poetae minores* (Garnier Frères, 1931), p. 324. He quotes two other lines of the same kind, dealing with the poets who interest us:

> Les Rimbaud et les Verlaine,
> Les reins beaux, ailés vers l'aine.

7. "Vers en assonances," *Chair*, Pléiade, p. 891; and "A la seule," *Invectives*, p. 958.

8. *CML*, I, 1265, letter to Ernest Raynaud of September 30, 1887.

9. *CML*, I, 1297.
10. To Jules Huret, *CML*, II, 1761.
11. *Ibid.*, p. 1760.
12. Quoted by Huret in his *Enquête*, p. 80.
13. Pléiade, 1074, and Martino, *op. cit.*, p. 188.
14. "J'ose espérer . . . que vous y reconnaîtrez, sinon le talent, du moins un effort vers . . . la Sensation rendue," letter of November 22, 1866. *CML*, I, 929.

Selected Bibliography

(Unless otherwise stated, the place of publication is Paris)

PRIMARY SOURCES

Verlaine's Works:

A. First Editions:

Poèmes saturniens, Alphonse Lemerre, 1866.
Les Amies, Sonnets par le licencié Pablo de Herlagnez, Ségovie/Brussels/, 1868.
Fêtes galantes, Alphonse Lemerre, 1869.
La Bonne Chanson, Alphonse Lemerre, 1870.
Romances sans paroles, Sens, Typographie de Maurice L'Hermitte, 1874.
Sagesse, Société générale de Librairie catholique, Ancienne maison Victor Palmé, 1881.
Jadis et Naguère, Léon Vanier, 1884.
Amour, Léon Vanier, 1888.
Parallèlement, Léon Vanier, 1889.
Dédicaces, Bibliothèque artistique et littéraire, 1890.
Femmes, imprimé sous le manteau et ne se vend nulle part, 1891.
Bonheur, Léon Vanier, 1891.
Chansons pour Elle, Léon Vanier, 1891.
Liturgies intimes, Bibliothèque du Saint-Graal, 1892.
Odes en son honneur, Léon Vanier, 1893.
Elégies, Lèon Vanier, 1893.
Dans les Limbes, Léon Vanier, 1894.
Epigrammes, Bibliothèque artistique et littéraire, 1894.
Chair, Bibliothèque artistique et littéraire, 1896.
Invectives, Léon Vanier, 1896.
Œuvres posthumes, Léon Vanier, 1903.
Hombres, imprimé sous le manteau et ne se vend nulle part, 1903 or 1904.

Biblio-sonnets, H. Floury, 1913.
Œuvres oubliées, Baudinière, 1926.

B. Collected Editions:

Œuvres complètes, Léon Vanier, 1899, reissued by Vanier's successor, Albert Messein. Five volumes.
Œuvres complètes, Club du Meilleur Livre, 1959-60. Two volumes. Until further notice, the definitive edition of Verlaine. Admirably done.
Œuvres poétiques complètes, Pléiade, 1966. Texte établi et annoté par Y. G. Le Dantec et Jacques Borel. Like most of the Pléiade volumes this one is a good example of how the French, during the last thirty or forty years, have beaten the Germans at their own game of text editing.
Œuvres libres de Paul Verlaine. Les Amies. Femmes. Hombres. Préface d'Etiemble. Au Cercle du Livre précieux, 1961.

SECONDARY SOURCES

ADAM, A. *Le Vrai Verlaine, essai psychanalytique.* Droz, 1936. An interesting study from the psychoanalytic point of view. Many sound conclusions.
________. *Verlaine.* Hatier, 1953. A useful summing-up.
ADAM, P. *Petit glossaire pour servir à l'intelligence des auteurs décadents et symbolistes.* Vanier, 1888. Useful for an understanding of Symbolist manias.
ARESSY, LUCIEN. *La Dernière Bohême, Verlaine et son milieu.* Jouve, no date. Anecdotes; some of them interesting.
BORNECQUE, J. H. *Etudies Verlainiennes, Les Poèmes saturniens.* Nizet, 1952.
________. *Lumières sur les Fêtes galantes.* Nizet, 1959. Both these volumes are excellent.
________. *Verlaine par lui-même,* Aux éditions du seuil.
CAZALS, F. A. and LE ROUGE, GASTON. *Les Derniers jours de Paul Verlaine.* Mercure de France, 1911. A valuable sketch of Verlaine's last years by two men who knew him well.
CARCO, FRANCIS. *Verlaine.* La Nouvelle Revue critique, 1939. A rather fictional treatment of the last years.
COULON, MARCEL. *Au Coeur de Verlaine et de Rimbaud.* Le Livre, 1925.
________. *Verlaine, poète saturnien.* Grasset, 1929. These two books were among the first to study Verlaine without reticence. Interesting documents. Tone a trifle dogmatic.
CUENOT, CLAUDE. *Etat présent des études verlainiennes.* Belles Lettres, 1938. Useful up to 1938.
DELAHAYE, ERNEST. *Verlaine.* Messein, 1923. A fundamental work,

particularly for the last half of Verlaine's life—after he met Rimbaud.

———. *Souvenirs familiers à propos de Rimbaud, Verlaine et Germain Nouveau.* Messein, 1925. As above.

DONOS, CHARLES. *Verlaine intime.* Vanier, 1898. Needs to be used with caution. Of some interest, however.

FONTAINAS, A. *Verlaine-Rimbaud, ce qu'on présume de leurs relations, ce qu'on en sait.* Librairie de France, 1931. Groups most of the documents but exhibits strange reticence in interpreting them.

GHIL, RENE. *Traité du Verbe.* Giraud, 1886. The lunatic fringe of Symbolism.

———. *Méthode Evolutive-Instrumentaliste d'une poésie rationnelle.* A. Savine, 1889. As above.

HUYSMANS, J. K. *A Rebours.* Charpentier-Fasquelle, 1884. Valuable and lasting criticism of Verlaine.

KAHN, GUSTAVE. *Symbolistes et Décadents.* Vanier, 1902. The lunatic fringe again. Most useful for an understanding of the period.

LE FEBVE DE VIVY, LEON. *Les Verlaine.* Miette, Bruxelles, 1928. Another fundamental work. The author seems to have had access to documents of great interest which, unfortunately, he does not always quote in full.

LEPELLETIER, EDMOND. *Paul Verlaine, sa vie, son oeuvre.* Mercure de France, 1907. The most important single work on Verlaine. Indispensable. Modern research has completed it in some ways.

LEMAITRE, JULES. *Les Contemporains.* Société française d'imprimerie et de Librairie, 1897, Vol. IV. Contains a study written for *La Revue bleue,* 7 janvier 1888, by one of the most influential pundits of the time.

MARTINO, P. *Verlaine, nouvelle édition revue et corrigée.* Boivin, 1951. Excellent summary.

MITCHELL, BONNER. *Les Manifestes littéraires de la belle époque.* Seghers, 1966. Literary manifestoes by Baju, Moréas, Gregh, etc.

MOREAS, J. *Esquisses et souvenirs.* Mercure de France, 1908. Confessions of a reformed Symbolist.

MORICE, CH. *Verlaine, l'homme et l'oeuvre.* Vanier, 1888. First study of Verlaine both as man and poet. Not of much interest.

MORICE, L. *Verlaine, Sagesse, édition critique commentée.* Nizet, 1964.

———. *Verlaine, le drame religieux.* Nizet, 1946. Excellent studies of the religious side of Verlaine's work.

MOUQUET, JULES. *Rimbaud raconté par Paul Verlaine.* Mercure de France, 1934. Useful anthology of extracts.

NADAL, O. *Paul Verlaine.* Mazenod, 1948.

———. PAUL VERLAINE. Mercure de France, 1961. M. Nadal is an

excellent critic, and whatever he says of Verlaine is worth attention. Profound and detailed discussions of Verlaine's poetry.

PORCHE, F. *Verlaine tel qu'il fut.* Flammarion, 1933. Still the best general life of Verlaine, but requires some correction.

RAYNAUD, E. *La Mêlée symboliste.* La Renaissance du Livre, 1920. Most valuable for background.

RICHER, J. *Paul Verlaine.* Seghers, 1960. A summary, with new points of view, many of them of great interest.

RIMBAUD, A. *Oeuvres complétes.* Pléiade, 1963. *Texte établi et annoté par Rolland de Renéville et Jules Mouquet.* Another fine Pléiade text.

———. *Correspondance 1888-1891, préface et notes de Jean Voellmy.* Gallimard, 1965. Rimbaud's letters from Abyssinia.

STARKIE, ENID. *Arthur Rimbaud.* New Directions, New York, 1960. The best study of Rimbaud in English.

TELLIER, JULES. *Nos Poètes.* Lecène et Oudin, 1889. Verlaine's milieu.

UNDERWOOD, V. P. *Verlaine et l'Angleterre.* Nizet, 1956. Magnificent piece of scholarship. Sets forth whatever contacts Verlaine had with England and clears up a number of obscure points.

VANWELKENHUYZEN, G. *Paul Verlaine en Belgique.* La Renaissance du Livre, Bruxelles, 1945. Important for Verlaine's contacts with Belgium.

VERLAINE, EX-MADAME PAUL (MATHILDE MAUTE). *Mémoires de ma vie. Précédés d'une introduction de M. François Porché.* Flammarion, 1935. With Lepelletier's book—and to a lesser extent Delahaye's—the most important document on Verlaine.

VICAIRE, G. *Les Déliquescences, poèmes décadents d'Adoré Floupette, avec sa vie par Marius Tapora.* Byzance, chez Lion Vanné, 1885. Amusing portrait of Verlaine as "Bleucoton." The Symbolist and Decadent milieu.

ZAYED, GEORGES. *Lettres inédites de Verlaine à Cazals.* Droz, Genève, 1957. Excellent and indispensable.

Articles:

BORNECQUE, J. H. "Les Dessous de Mémoires d'un veuf," *Revue des sciences humaines* (avril-juin, 1952).

BOUGARD, P. "La Famille maternelle de Verlaine d'après les archives du Pas-de-Calais," *Revue des Sciences humaines* (avril-juin, 1952).

DECADENCE, LA. Secrétaire de la rédaction René Ghil, 1886.

DECADENT, LE. Directeur A. Baju, 1886-1889.

ERMITAGE, L'. Février, 1902, "Quel est votre poète?" Order of preferences resulting from the inquiry: Hugo, Vigny, Verlaine, Baudelaire, Lamartine, etc.

GIRAUD, ALBERT. "Les Poètes baudelairiens," *La Jeune Belgique*, Bruxelles (avril, 1888).

KESSLER, HARRY GRAF. *Besuch bei Verlaine*. Insel-Almanach, 1965. Contains a number of interesting remarks.

MARTIN, AUGUSTE. "Verlaine et Rimbaud," *Nouvelle Revue Française* (février, 1943). The Verlaine dossier from the Préfecture de Police. Important.

RODENBACH, G. "La Poésie nouvelle. A propos des décadents et des symbolistes," *La Revue bleue* (4 avril 1891). Verlaine's position with advanced literary groups of the period.

VERHAEREN, E. "Paul Verlaine," *la Revue Blanche* (15 avril 1897). As above.

Index

DATE DUE

GAYLORD			PRINTED IN U.S.A